Marnie

With many thanks
and good wishes

Audrie Thompson-Guppy

class of '68.

Stepmothers

Stepmothers
Exploring the Myth

Kati Morrison, M.D.
and
Airdrie Thompson-Guppy
with
Patricia Bell

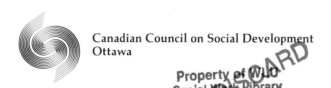

Canadian Council on Social Development
Ottawa

Canadian Cataloguing in Publication Data

    Morrison, Kati
    Stepmothers

    Bibliography: p.
    ISBN 0-88810-358-1 (bound). —
    ISBN 0-88810-357-3 (pbk.)

    1. Stepmothers—Canada.
    2. Stepfamilies—Canada.
    I. Thompson-Guppy, Airdrie   II. Bell, Pat
    III. Canadian Council on Social Development
    IV. Title.

    HQ759.92.M67 1985   646.7'8   C86-090004-5

Printed and bound in Canada by Love Printing Services Ltd.

The Canadian Council on Social Development
55 Parkdale Ave.
P.O. Box 3505, Station C
Ottawa, Ontario K1Y 4G1

Cover art: Janice Street
Inside Illustrations: Aniko Barta

To my stepchildren Diana and Rob who in a web of conflicting expectations have succeeded both in being loyal to all the adults in their family and in benefiting from all who care about them.

Kati Morrison

To Louise, Marjorie and Claydon: towards an understanding of the years we shared together; and,

To Allison and Gordon for sharing me with another family.

Airdrie Thompson-Guppy

A note on the case histories.

The names and places cited in the case histories described in this book are all fictional. However, they have all been reconstructed from actual cases.

CONTENTS

Stepfamilies are here to stay and they are growing in numbers. But even the official Canadian census ignores their existence. Second marriages often founder because of conflicts over the children. Since society is still not comfortable with the notion of stepfamilies, members may find it easier to pose as a nuclear family for a time. However, denying reality won't work. Step-parenting can be successful, but you can't go it alone.

Women are still expected to take on the primary responsibility for children. For a stepmother, however, the frustrations and satisfactions are very different from those experienced by a natural mother. The Cinderella myth is still with us, including the misconception that natural mothers are all loving and caring while stepmothers are all wicked. In fact, many stepmothers attempt to be Supermoms; they offer themselves as surrogates and end up as scapegoats. This chapter is a frank and intensive look at what it means to be a stepmother today.

Children can be badly hurt by the strife surrounding the separation of their parents. Their trust in adults is shaken as they learn that the two people whom they most love and need don't want to live together any longer. This chapter examines the needs and behavior of children of various ages at the time of their parents' divorce and subsequent remarriage. A child's bond with his or her own mother is fundamental and she can continue to provide strong emotional support even though living apart.

Chapter Three: Structure of Stepfamilies and Legal Issues

A stepfamily is born of the loss of an earlier relationship, either through divorce or death, and it can take several forms. Whether it consists of a man, a woman and her children; a man, a woman and his children; or a couple who both bring children to the new marriage, it is a stepfamily. It's also a stepfamily whether some or all of the children live with the couple, or whether they visit regularly or sporadically. This chapter provides a clear picture of a stepfamily. The economic responsibility of both natural parents for their children is also discussed in this chapter, along with suggestions for institutional reforms. Often custody arrangements change as children grow or circumstances alter. Carried out without recourse to the courts, no records are kept, and official statistics on child custody don't tell the whole story.

Chapter Four: The Extended Family

Stepchildren are not orphans. Quite the contrary. Sometimes it seems they have more relatives than they can sort out. These people—including grandparents, aunts and uncles—can help with the step-parenting. This chapter describes the variety an extended family can bring, and the benefits to children of feeling at home in several settings.

Chapter Five: Discipline—Whose Responsibility?

Two adults who have decided to be parents together must both set reasonable limits on children's behavior. This important chapter offers some realistic guidelines.

Chapter Six: Special Events

Whether it's seating arrangements at a graduation ceremony, the baptism of a stepgrandchild, or the logistics of celebrating Christmas in two households, members of stepfamilies can find special events more painful than special. This chapter examines some of the complexities, noting the identity confusion of being a parent and a non-parent, a relative and a stranger, and feeling proud and superfluous all at the same time.

Parenting in any form is a maturing experience. Looking back on several years of being stepmothers, it's possible to see that there are some issues or feelings that won't ever change. There are also many positive experiences that have allowed the stepchildren to grow into independent young adults. For stepmothers, the realization that they have made a vital contribution is one reward.

Foreword

Diane is a wicked stepmother. A highly sophisticated, perfectly groomed woman seated next to her beautiful, intelligent and articulate natural daughter, she has been haranguing her stepson David for the last half-hour. While David's father, Joe, squirms uncomfortably, David, a slightly obese and verbally awkward 15-year-old boy, stares morosely at his feet. Diane accuses David of being a liar, a manipulator and of having no feelings or concern for anyone but himself. David's futile attempts to defend himself are interrupted by Diane, who by now is screaming that David is going to be the cause of the breakup of this second marriage.

Diane gives Joe an ultimatum. "Choose between me or David! " David's father and stepmother bring him to the psychiatrist so that he may be declared mentally disturbed and placed in a residential treatment facility. With David temporarily removed from the family, the couple hopes to re-establish a strong marital bond. Alternatively, this marriage, like 47 per cent of other Canadian second marriges, will fail.

Stepmothers: Exploring the Myth, written for and by stepmothers, helps the reader to see Diane's "wickedness" differently. Diane's dilemma is presented early in chapter one. The authors show how stepmothers who attempt to become Supermoms or surrogate mothers may end up as scapegoats. In dispelling the myth of the wicked stepmother, the authors also challenge the belief of many stepmothers that the more they give, the better life will be. Having carefully explained and illustrated the fallacy of such a belief system, the authors offer alternative courses of action. At the end of each chapter, behavioral guidelines are presented for all members of the stepfamily.

Stepchildren are not forgotten. In chapter two, for example, the authors eloquently illustrate the difficulties experienced by the members of a stepfamily. Each member may be at a different stage in mourning the loss of the nuclear family, coping with the remarriage, and entering into a stepfamily.

Dr. Kati Morrison, staff psychiatrist, and Mrs. Airdrie Thompson-Guppy, the Director of Social Work, both at the Queensway-Carleton Hospital in Ottawa, bring to this work their professional experiences working with stepfamilies. As a result of two previous research projects, they have described a syndrome, unique to stepmothers, which includes the following symptoms: 1) identity confusion; 2) sense of helplessness with ineffective coping skills; 3) exhaustion/burn-out; 4) feelings of inadequacy; 5) anger at rejection; and 6) anxiety.

This syndrome which they call "Cinderella's Stepmother's Syndrome" was first described in a paper presented to the Seventh World Congress of Psychiatry in Vienna, Austria, in July, 1983. The syndrome appears to be an adjustment reaction with depressive features and anxiety.

In addition to their professional background, these authors' personal experiences as stepmothers enhance their understanding and empathy. They see stepmothers as women who are adjusting to this role as well as responding to changes in the current Canadian view of the traditional female role of caregiver in the family.

What makes this book unique is the authors' refusal to allow their empathy and identification to color their perception of the common errors made by stepmothers. If, as a stepmother, you expect this book to confirm and compliment you on your martyrdom to your husband's children, you will be disappointed. Alternatively, if you are really seeking to develop an appropriate relationship with your stepchildren, separate and different from that enjoyed by their natural mother, then this book will more than fulfill your expectations.

The authors tell us that most stepmothers *do* understand that the children in their care will love their natural mother most. However, many of the fathers and stepmothers whom I see in my child psychiatric practice appear to have forgotten this basic premise. They are not alone. Extended family members, friends, and even trained professionals often treat the members of a stepfamily as if they were members of a nuclear family.

Several weeks ago, I went to a meeting at Heather's school to discuss her progress. While waiting for her stepfather and mother to arrive, I thoughtlessly enquired, "Do your father and mother know where to meet us?" She swung furiously towards me and shouted, "He's not my father!" Heather, age 16, is recovering from a major depressive episode during which she made a serious suicide attempt. Now, in a special school, she is achieving well for the first time since grade two, and is beginning to develop friendships with the other students. Her parents separated when she was three, and her brother Bill just one year old. Her father's career necessitates that he move frequently. His contact with his children over the years has been sporadic and inconsistent. Heather's stepfather is a university professor; his two teenage daughters, who live with their mother, are brilliant academic and music students. Several years ago, her stepfather had openly admitted defeat in trying to help Heather with her schooling.

Heather remains strongly attached to her biological parent. This bond is an ambivalent one that encompasses much anger and interferes with her developing new bonds with her stepfather.

Heather's difficulties illustrate for me the central theme so well described in this work: a stepfamily and the inter-relationships in a stepfamily are very different from those in a nuclear family. The stepmother's and the stepfather's attachment or bonding with the child is very different from that of the biological parent. While the family may appear similar to a nuclear family, it must not be viewed or treated as such.

In this text, the authors make a significant contribution to primary prevention of the development of adverse reaction. By "unmasking" the stepfamily, they have made us all aware of the need to see beyond the "masquerading" as a nuclear family and to explore the alternate coping strategies they offer.

B. E. Robson, M.D., F.R.C.P.(C)

Dr. Bonnie Robson is assistant professor at the Department of Psychiatry, University of Toronto, staff psychiatrist at the Hincks Treatment Center and a private psychiatrist as well. She is the author of My Parents are Divorced Too *and she is directing extensive research regarding the effect of divorce on children.*

Preface

This is a book that grew through the years. It all began with a friendly chat, grew to a mutual support group, and soon expanded through professional channels to incorporate discussions with some 300 stepmothers.

Our thoughts and impressions intimidated some of our colleagues, but patients and friends who were experiencing step-relationships readily nodded and smiled as our work began to outline etiquette and protocol for second marriage families.

The discoveries of common pain, problems and humorous, constructive ways to weather stepfamily hurdles, were the shared experience of the authors with another colleague, Fiona Faucher. We have fond memories of those pioneer times trying to understand the issues of stepmotherhood, and we express our appreciation of Fiona's valuable contribution to these intense and enlightening experiences.

To those people who did believe in us, our warmest thanks for helping us to pursue our dream. Our dream is to enable stepmothers to hold their heads high and acknowledge that they are indeed who they are—women caring for and helping to raise their husband's natural children. Though presented from the stepmother's perspective, this work applies to all stepfamily members and their friends.

The first written piece came from Kati's mother, Judit Jozsef, when we discovered the lack of a positive and good stepmother in fairy tales and literature in general. We thank her for the *The King's Choice*—the challenge of the myth.

Our mentor Jonathan Williams helped us tremendously by his invaluable advice and encouragement, and mainly by his faith in us, and in the idea that we had something original and important to say. We just had to find a way to express it.

This "way" became possible only after we invited Pat Bell to help us put our thoughts into her enjoyable, clear and rich style. Her patience, as well as her genuine interest, were most needed and appreciated. As the person in our group who is not a stepmother but has a great deal of experience in parenting and writing about it, she contributed to our dialogue.

Kati's husband, Bob Morrison, contributed to the thorough editing and revising of the manuscript. Both Bob, and Airdrie's husband, Jack Guppy, contributed their particular perspective as custodial fathers. Their support and trust in us was essential for this highly charged project. Their loyalty was greatly tested in helping us through.

Airdrie's uncle, John Bell, must also be acknowledged for his unfailing interest and encouragement throughout the trials and tribulations of this project.

We were most fortunate to find Aniko Barta, who captured our messages in delightful and uncomplicated illustrations for the book. She was able to combine both the humorous and the serious in drawings that expressed what words alone could not always convey.

Our respective employers, Queensway-Carleton Hospital and Children's Hospital of Eastern Ontario, both in Ottawa, were most supportive of our endeavor, with both hospital libraries and particularly the Psychiatric Department at Q.C.H. offering us their knowledge.

Betty Ann Cory and Eugenia Kanellakos provided an invaluable service in quickly typing revisions to our manuscript and enabling us to meet deadlines.

Secretarial assistance from Verna Garrard at C.H.E.O., Sharon Ingram and Gillian Weatherall from Q.C.H., and Airdrie's mother, Joan Bell, was also particularly appreciated.

The King's Choice

In a small and peaceful kingdom, not so long ago nor far away, lived a royal family that appeared to be very happy. The King and Queen both loved their daughter who was blessed not only with beauty but also with a kind and gentle spirit.

Her beauty she inherited from her mother, but in temperament they were very different. The Queen was harsh and bitter in spite of the unceasing efforts of everyone to please her. No error on the part of a servant went unnoticed nor unpunished and, as time went by, not even the King or Princess could escape the Queen's angry tongue.

Whether the King had been discussing affairs of state with his court officials or had been away from the castle for days tending to his people's concerns, he could never be sure of a warm welcome on his return. Instead, the Queen would greet him in a scolding tone, ordering him not to enter her flower-filled room in his wrinkled, sweat-stained clothes. "You can't sit down here, like this," she would say. "I am the Queen, don't forget."

Because the King loved his wife he tried to conform to her wishes. But after several years of her nagging, the long-suffering King could take it no more.

"My dear wife", he said, "I know that you love me and that you are a good woman. However, you are not suited to be the Queen and my partner. I am going to send you away from the Royal Palace and then I shall search for another wife who is able to behave in a kinder manner toward me, toward our daughter, and toward all the members of the household."

The Queen had no choice but to leave. Although she was saddened, she also knew that all her needs would be met generously by the King for the rest of her life.

In due course, the King began to consider whom he should take as his second wife. From among the thousands of women who would have been happy to fill the role, he picked three possible choices. Before he would decide on one of these, he had to know which woman would make the appropriate stepmother for his daughter.

One by one, they were led into the princess' room while the King watched them from a secret window. The first woman said to the daughter, "Tell your father, the King, that if he marries me, you will have the loveliest wardrobe in the whole world. Nobody will look as beautiful as you."

The second woman didn't promise anything about beauty. Instead, she offered learning. "Tell your father, the King, that if he marries me, I will make sure that you are taught by the very wisest of teachers. Brilliant artists will share the secrets of their skills with you and you shall be the brightest and best educated young woman in the whole world."

When the third woman entered the princess' room, she simply said "Hello" and waited for the little girl to begin the conversation. This surprised the princess, who wondered why she wasn't hearing more promises.

"I'm not going to make grand promises," this woman said quietly. "But if it happens that in the future I may live near you, whether or not your father, the King, chooses to marry me, I should like to help you to grow up to be a true human being."

"And what about the beautiful dresses?" the child asked.

"You'll learn to take care of yourself and to make the most of your beauty, but appearance is not the most important thing in life," was the reply.

"And what about art and literature and learning from wise teachers?" the princess asked again.

"Yes, you will study too," the woman answered: "But what you will find is that the most important thing in life is realizing your potential as a human being."

"What does that mean?" the princess exclaimed, bewildered.

"You can only understand with time, but it means to help others, to learn to take care of yourself while enjoying companionship, and to develop strong friendships through kindness."

The King, listening to such unusual talk, decided to ask this woman to be his wife and the stepmother to his daughter. She was true to her word, and under her guidance, the princess grew up happy, self-reliant and a joy to all who knew her.

The princess came to appreciate and trust her stepmother, although she still loved her mother most. For her part, the stepmother knew that her relationship with the princess would never be exactly that of a mother and daughter, but she felt satisfied that their life together was happy and she knew that her efforts were worthwhile.

Years later, after a series of natural disasters and wars, the King lost much of his wealth. However, the princess was prepared to find a fulfilling job and to earn her own living. Her early training also helped her to dress in a most becoming manner on a very small budget. As is to be expected in fairy tales, one day a kind and handsome prince asked her to marry him. And she did.

The princess lived a long and happy life, eventually becoming a Queen herself. Through the years she maintained faithful ties to her father, her mother and her stepmother. If anyone ever mentioned the terms "wicked stepmother" or "cruel stepmother," she would ask in sincere wonder: "What are those?"

Introduction

This book is about stepfamilies. It is written from the stepmother's perspective, but it is not just *about* stepmothers, nor just *for* stepmothers. We hope it will be useful to everyone who wants to understand more about stepfamilies.

When a woman marries a man with children, she is a stepmother, whether the children live with her, see her only on holidays, or never see her at all from one year's end to the next. Since 1973, more than 500,000 children have been affected by divorce, and 75 per cent of single parents remarry. According to projections in a Statistics Canada study, by the end of the 1980s almost half of Canadian families will be of the remarried form.

In 85 per cent of divorces involving children, custody is awarded to the mother. However, for a variety of reasons, including the fact that on average women earn much less than men, a large proportion of these children end up spending all or part of their growing years with their father, without the courts' knowledge or involvement.

Although scant attention in research has been paid to remarriage, statistical trends indicate that the remarriage rate is rising. The most common pattern of remarriage is a single man and a divorced woman (26.7 per cent); a divorced man and a single woman (23 per cent); and, a divorced man and a divorced woman (20 per cent). Widowed persons are much less likely to remarry; as a result, 70 per cent of remarriages involved divorced persons.

Stepfamilies are an institution in our society. They are here to stay, and they are growing in number. It must also be noted, however, that remarriages between divorced persons are more apt to end in divorce than first marriages. The principal reason second marriages fail appears to be trouble over children from a first marriage as Kay Pasley, Assistant

Professor of Family Studies, reported at the 1984 meeting of the Orthopsychiatrists Association. She drew that conclusion after reviewing the literature relating to remarried families. If stepfamilies could recognize themselves as a unique family form that is completely different from the original, nuclear family, they will have an opportunity for greater stability.

We will use the term "nuclear family" to describe a family where two parents live with their own children only. One of this book's main themes is that stepfamilies are very different from nuclear families, even though they may appear the same to outsiders. Indeed, recognition of the differences is an important key to the formation of an effective and harmonious stepfamily.

Realistic expectations can lessen the stress that currently leads to a dissolution rate of 47 per cent for second marriages.

The scarcity of studies and investigations of the stepfamily is an indication of society's failure to give stepfamilies the recognition their numbers deserve. Even an exact count of those numbers is not available. During the latest Canadian official government census (1981), individuals were asked about sixteen different relationships that people in one household might have with each other, including "lodger's son/daughter." No mention was made of stepchild, stepfather or stepmother.

Helping to raise someone else's children in a remarried family is not the stuff little girls dream of when they fantasize about their future. It is one of those "couldn't happen to me" situations. But if there are three daughters in your household today, chances are one of them will become a stepmother.

For a stepmother to admit that she cannot recommend the role to her own daughter without some reservations is not easy, nor is it pleasant to acknowledge that being a stepmother is one of the more frustrating experiences in life. But it is the truth, and once stated, it is possible to go on to examine the opportunities for good times and great satisfactions that also come with being a step-parent.

Stepfamilies, and stepmothers in particular, have been almost invisible for a long time. We wrote this book because we believe second marriages can survive, and individuals can be enriched by the stepfamily experience. Stepmothers can find fulfilling companionship with their husbands, while finding the rearing of someone else's kids to be a worthwhile and important challenge.

We hope to help demystify the stepfamily pattern and, by examining what makes up a stepfamily, we want to share some helpful norms and guidelines. We will focus on the responsibilities of both natural parents, as well as those of other members of the children's extended family. We will look at discipline and caring for each other. We also offer a guide to understanding the stepmother who cares for children on a day-by-day basis. She cannot possibly hope to help repair some of the damage that happened before she came on the scene, nor to make right everything in the present situation without the cooperation of her husband and the children in the household, as well as the natural parent outside the home.

Why is it so difficult? Why does there have to be conflict and pain in a situation where the new stepmother simply wants to help, and the children obviously need to be cared for? Most books generalize or shy away from these questions, suggesting that if step-parents just try harder to please everyone, things will go more smoothly. That will not work. Step-parenting can be successful, but the stepmother cannot do it alone. Stepmothers need and deserve some help.

First of all, the extended family, that is the child's non-custodial parent and relatives, has a responsibility to care for the well-being of the child. That responsibility does not end with divorce and remarriage. A beloved grandfather or aunt cannot simply exit from a child's life because a stepmother has entered the picture. These people are not interchangeable pieces in a child's life.

A husband cannot assume that a smooth adjustment will just happen between his children and the woman who is now a parent with him. This has to be a cooperative venture; not all the adjusting has to be done by her. After all, the husband is the family member with the responsibility for the previous marriage, and the children from that marriage.

The natural mother still has a very important role to play. Rather than washing her hands of responsibilities if she does not have custody, then feeling deprived of her maternal role, she must realize that her children still need her and will always put her first in their affections. Even though she is not with them on a daily basis, she does have a tremendous effect on their growth and development.

Institutions such as schools and churches also have a responsibility to offer support to stepfamilies, rather than ignoring them or treating them exactly the same as nuclear families.

The relative obscurity of the stepfamily is one of its most pervasively destructive elements. Although society appears to favor remarriages, it stops short of recognizing or supporting them as stepfamilies. If the Canadian census ignores them, it should not be a surprise that children in reconstituted families often avoid telling anyone they have a step-parent. Divorces and single-parent families are recognized and counted, but the "happily ever after" that did not happen in the first marriage is nonetheless supposed to magically occur in the second. The need for support services to assist members of a stepfamily learn to live together amicably has not received much attention. Until recently, it was common legal practice to declare one parent "unfit," with the expectation that this person would disappear forever from the child's life. This departure of the "superfluous" parent would then allow the custodial parent to remarry and take up the model of the neat, nuclear family. In cases where the other person is still very much a part of the child's life, society does not yet comfortably recognize this fact. Pretending to be an original nuclear family means denying the existence of several persons who can still affect the new marriage. This creates stresses and strains on everyone, especially the children. At the same time, assuming that a remarried family can immediately function as a homogeneous, intact unit is not entirely fair. It takes time for adjustments to occur. For too long stepfamilies have tried to adapt to this nuclear family model, rather than working out their own way of doing things based on the authentic expectations of all the people involved, including those who do not live under the new family roof.

Stepfamilies are born out of the loss of an earlier relationship, through divorce or death. Adults and children have to go through a grieving process before they feel free to adjust to the lifestyle of a new family. There is a special bond between the child and parent that flourished while they were on their own. And there continues to be an influence on the child by the natural parent who is living apart which cannot be controlled by the adults in the household. An important theme of this book is that in almost all cases children form a very powerful bond to their mothers during their early years. Even abused or neglected children cling to their mothers for nurture. The stepmother enjoys no such deep-rooted attachment. On the contrary, she comes on the scene as an outsider. She is often seen as taking the rightful place of the mother, even if she had no role in the divorce.

Most of our advice is based on the assumption that the biological parents accord a priority to their children's welfare and are capable of cooperating in the children's interest. In these cases, we advocate continuing close contact between the children and the non-custodial parent, and a responsible role for the latter in parenting. Where a parent does not accord prime consideration to the children's interest, where hatred toward the former partner is a dominant factor, or where there is mental breakdown, it may be necessary to limit contact with the natural parent.

Studies show that children do well if they are able to maintain good relationships with both parents after a divorce occurs, regardless of the discomfort this may cause the adults.

A new step-parent, even with the best of intentions, cannot take the place of caring relatives who may become lost to children when their parents divorce and remarry. An awareness and understanding of the dynamics of the stepfamily is essential to ensure that all members participate and benefit to the extent possible from the new links they are forging. For example, no traditions have yet been developed to tell us how to fit grandparents and other members of the child's extended family into a network of caring adults to whom he or she can turn. There are bound to be problems in adjusting to a new family situation, and they cannot be solved through silence.

Yet silence is still one of the most common responses to the many questions facing stepfamilies. Just because two adults fall in love and decide to marry does not mean that his children will happily accept her, or that her children will feel like calling him dad. There is no reason for new stepbrothers and stepsisters to automatically take to each other either.

Society appears to prefer to believe that with remarriage, all is well under one roof again. It is not that simple. The history of divorce and single living is not suddenly forgotten. The newly found emotional attachment between the adults does not necessarily mean that the children will share in the glow. Their needs may not be completely met within the new blended family, and it is important for them to have the assurance that both natural parents still love them. Research on children of divorce has shown consistently that there are both short and long-term reactions. Increased behavior problems—aggressiveness in boys and delinquency in both boys and girls—have been reported in professional literature. To the outsider, the family structure of mother, father and children may look familiar, but a stepfamily is not a nuclear family. Masquerading as one means that every member must be an actor, and that cannot go on indefinitely in the real world.

Intelligent people who have managed successfully in other areas of life are distressed by their inability to handle step-parenting with ease. An ever-increasing number are coming to mental health facilities because of problems related to unsettled issues in stepfamily relationships, and some of these issues linger to affect even the second and third generations.

Meeting more and more of stepfamily "casualties" in our daily work, and becoming stepmothers ourselves, heightened our interest in the subject. But it was not until we got past socially acceptable pleasantries and actually admitted that we found being a stepmother a sometimes perplexing position that we could really begin to examine what was happening.

This book blends our personal experience and understanding as stepmothers with our professional contacts with families facing similar adjustments.

It was Airdrie's spontaneous remark shortly after her remarriage, "it's tough being a stepmother," that prompted Kati to suggest getting together with others in similar situations to share common concerns and insights.

Meeting frequently over the next three years, we found that talking things through together helped tremendously, both personally and professionally. Together and separately, we had discussions with about 300 stepfamilies. The examples raised throughout this book are based upon actual situations and events, but the names and locations have been changed to protect the privacy of the individuals involved.

Preparing and presenting workshops on stepfamilies to a wide variety of professional groups made us aware of the growing number of people with a stepfamily connection. Participants were looking not only for guidance in assisting families with whom they were working, but also for answers to difficulties within their own households or to long-standing problems with a step-parent.

While stumbling along in self-imposed isolation, we had assumed that our difficulties were our own individual problems. It was a relief to discover that they were common. We all understood pains, doubts and bad feelings each had experienced. Following a *Globe and Mail* article early in 1980 about our families and our work, we found others who felt the same way. A father of three phoned seeking a counselling source for his wife. As a stepmother, she had experienced occasional difficulties, but had always felt she should be able to manage on her own. Reading that we had found strength in helping each other, she too was now ready to look for support.

A young woman read the article and recalled that she had given her stepmother a hard time many years before. As a teenager she had left her natural mother to move in with her father and his new wife. "I was fifteen and I decided that I'd had enough of my mother's rules. My stepmother was a wonderful person, but I was a rotten kid. Do you think it's too late to go back and tell her that I really love her and appreciate what she did for me?"

When we were invited to participate in a radio hotline show in Montreal, we realized that not one stepmother phoned in during that whole hour.

The relatives, particularly the stepchildren, who did call, all had unresolved conflicts with stepfamily relationships, and in every case the natural mother was excused for anything she had done or not done. We became more determined than ever to speak out about stepfamilies.

The word "stepmother" itself is not associated with thoughts of care, understanding and nurturing. Yet most stepmothers are taking on this daily care of children while fighting within themselves the myth of the wicked stepmother well-known to readers of fairy tales. Being made to feel like a foreign body that the family wants very much to reject does not seem fair compensation for all that cooking, shopping, driving, nursing and planning. Stepmothers do understand that the children will love their natural mother most in the world. We ask in return that natural mothers allow their children to recognize the contribution the stepmother is making to their welfare.

We believe that it is possible to enjoy life as a member of a stepfamily; we hope by addressing the realities and confronting some of the problems, this book will contribute to a growing number of individuals who find they can agree.

Chapter One

Stepmothers—Looking Past The Label

When Eileen met Ben, she had three teenagers of her own, so adding his two young daughters to the family outings was more fun than work when they got together. Through three years of courtship, the couple and five children had enjoyed camping, cycling, lots of movies, and easy-going television and popcorn evenings at Eileen's house. Ben would then take his daughters home. Their daily routine was his responsibility.

Not until the marriage and the move to a big house for everyone was there any concrete talk of rules and expectations. Then reality set in. The party time was over; dishwashing schedules, homework and curfews became a regular source of arguments.

When Eileen's nursing staff colleagues at the hospital noticed their peppy, competent friend more quiet than usual, and enquired how the new family arrangement was working out, she had to admit it was not proving to be easy. Eileen was becoming sad and beginning to feel like a stepmother.

How is it possible that an optimistic, outgoing, capable person thrust into a stepmother role, would suddenly turn into a woman with a low opinion of her abilities and a tendency to withdraw from others rather than to ask for help?

A stepmother may not quite be an acquisition to brag about, as one would a new bike or a baby brother, but neither is she the nobody she may be made to feel like when teenagers would "rather die" than introduce her to their schoolmates.

It's important to take a special look at the stepmother role because it has a large impact on the health and well-being of the entire blended family. The stepfather's role seems to have a different meaning. This is perhaps because it is still true that the mothering experience is a more crucial element of a woman's life and sense of self-worth than is the father role for a man. When a man marries a woman with children, her friends and relatives may breathe a huge sigh of relief now that the family is complete again in their eyes—they will be "taken care of." But they do not expect the new stepfather to check the children's homework, make their dental appointments, be home every night to tuck them into bed and so on. Society continues to expect that sort of dedication from a mother. All too often she expects it of herself.

Stepmothers often expect too much of themselves, fighting the pervasive myth of the wicked stepmother on the one hand, and the myth of the all-caring, all-loving natural mother on the other. This latter concept of the instinctive maternal figure is being challenged in today's society as more and more mothers begin to excuse themselves from striving to be perfect. Unfortunately this more easy-going attitude has not yet been adopted for stepmothers. They are still expected to pick up where the natural mother left off, with children who still need mothering.

New stepmothers, unable to foresee the pitfalls, and often bolstered by a proven record in facing other challenges, easily step right into the trap and mistakenly assume that the more they do, and the more they give, the better it will be for everyone in the family. Not so. The best defence is to take it slow, look around and assess the situation before plunging into action. Taking on the mantle of stepmother is very different from becoming a biological mother and, contrary to popular belief, the stepmother never takes the place of the natural mother. She becomes a new member of a new family, not a replacement part in the old one. The bonds and intimacy of the mother-child relationship are not there for her; her task involves guiding young people toward responsible adulthood, without any proprietary rights.

In almost all cases, children form a powerful bond with their mothers. Of course this biological tie is not available to the stepmother. She comes on the scene as an outsider, even though she comes with good will. Stepfamilies may resemble nuclear families in their pattern of two adults and children, but the key to building an effective stepfamily is to recognize that it is *not* a nuclear family, where two parents live with their children and no one else's.

A stepmother needs time, patience and a willingness to build a positive relationship with children who are not interested in having anyone take their mother's place.

In this chapter we shall examine what is involved in being a stepmother. We will begin by considering the attributes of women who choose to take on the task and the goals they have in mind. Then we will observe the characteristics of the many stepmothers who find that their hopes are not being realized. For a large number, disappointment and disillusionment come because they had no idea the situation would be so complex. The issues that make it this way form the next part of the chapter, and help to explain why stepmothers often lose a great deal of their enthusiasm and self-esteem. Coping with conflicts and petty irritations on a daily basis can get in the way of the positive things the stepmother may want to bring to her new family. The problem is to learn how to rechannel her energies, something she cannot do until she takes a candid look at her relationship with her husband, his children and their natural mother. Once these relationships have been brought into a realistic focus, there are many positive things to be said about the stepmothering experience.

Who marries a man with children?

In all likelihood, she will be a woman who feels that life with someone else's children will not be too complicated. Women who see children as an unavoidable burden are not likely to stay in the picture.

Women who become stepmothers are well aware that the closeness and companionship they are seeking with another adult will be influenced by the irreversible fact that there are children to consider. The couple bond is primary to them, but a ready-made family as part of the package may be considered a bonus. Whether or not it's a spoken motivation, the woman who marries a man with children wants to help bring them up.

Sometimes it's a woman who does not have children of her own. She may not want to go through a pregnancy, or may be unable to, and welcomes the thought of children through marriage. If she does have her own children, she probably enjoyed the motherhood experience and thinks she will be good at being a stepmother. Another advantage to her marrying this man is that he will have had experience acting as a father figure. As well, coping with children on his own may demonstrate the very skills and sensitivities that she is seeking in a partner.

Our work with such women over a number of years, and our ever-widening circle of acquaintances and colleagues who have become stepmothers, lead us to describe the person who does so in the following way. She is most likely an individual who enjoys helping others and gets along well with people. She is outgoing, has many friends and varied interests, and takes time to enjoy them. She is known as a competent worker with a mature sense of responsibility and a high frustration tolerance. On top of that, she likes children.

Most of the women who choose to become stepmothers look forward to the experience because nothing in their lives up to this point has suggested that they cannot handle it well. What, then, can turn some of these optimistic, practical women into bitter, frustrated, hostile creatures who find the task overwhelming? We believe it is a combination of the complexity of the role itself, and unrealistic expectations.

Stepmothers who do seek help are beginning to realize that they cannot do everything themselves. Of the many stepmothers we have seen, many share similar characteristics. The most important include: low self-esteem; reluctance to ask for help; tendency to overprotect other members of the family; difficulty setting limits for children's behavior; and, fear of rejection.

For many stepmothers, life at work and elsewhere outside the family goes on much as before, including the same camaraderie with friends and colleagues. But at home, where so much of their emotions and energies are invested, they are seen differently. For some, this can mean living in a house with round-the-clock hostility. Being able to foresee some of the issues involved in step-parenting, before the marriage takes place, could help women approach their new role more realistically, including an appropriate awareness of the need for a strong sense of self-preservation.

Things a stepmother should know...beforehand

First of all, in the eyes of the stepchildren, the stepmother may not be seen as the person she really is. They may have either resentments about this intruder, or very high expectations of what she can do. Most often they will have both. Sensing a gap that needs to be filled, a new wife and stepmother may throw herself into this role of provider so thoroughly that she obscures the real person inside. Later, when she becomes weary and wishes to change her role, nobody seems interested in her other talents or the things that are important to her. Such cool indifference is easier to face if a stepmother has not been trying to force herself into a mould to suit everyone else's convenience, and has been able from the beginning to maintain a little distance from the children and their demands.

Because the motherhood role is a fulfilling experience for many women, and because a number of women judge their own self-worth by their success as mothers, it may feel natural for a stepmother to attempt to gain a sense of satisfaction from doing a great job with the stepchildren.

Unfortunately, there are many factors beyond her control, including everything that happened before she came on the scene, and the fact that the children have other adults, and often a mother, who care for them. A stepmother, despite the word, is not a substitute for the children's mother. Any satisfaction she derives from helping children progress through life can be reasonably compared to that of a teacher towards a pupil, or any other responsible adult who invests time and thought into helping others take constructive steps in their lives.

In return for that concern and care, a stepmother is entitled to respect. What she cannot expect is the type of family bond that allows her to make mistakes without fear of being harshly judged. A natural parent can do that, and even administer strict discipline, because the biological tie and memories of good times allow for it. A stepmother, however, is observed more closely and judged more harshly for *perceived* errors.

One of the most frustrating things for a stepmother is wanting to help her stepchildren, knowing they need help, but being constantly rebuffed. One stepmother likens the experience to that of bumping against a glass wall, with the children reaching out their hands on one side, while she offers hers on the other, but the glass is constantly in the way, frustrating a direct encounter. One familiar form of this conflict between needs and a desire to help is the rejection by children of meals prepared by the stepmother.

Children need the opportunity to keep in touch with their natural mother and to know that she still loves them. Without this confidence that their mother is still available to them, stepchildren often demonstrate their sense of loss through hostility toward the stepmother. Attempts by the stepmother to encourage affection and closeness in the children can give rise to loyalty conflicts and feelings of guilt.

Trying to make up to the children for the pain they feel is too big a task for the stepmother. It belongs more appropriately to the children's father, and perhaps also to other members of the family. A stepmother will find that she has to learn to live with a dominant shadow, the children's natural mother and her husband's former wife, who is not going to disappear from everyone's memory so the stepmother can feel more at ease and pretend she is living in a neat little nuclear family. That's just not going to happen. The natural mother is a part of the children's family and will always be, whether or not she shares in the parenting, sees the children on a regular basis, or tries to avoid any responsibility. Whatever she chooses to do, she will have an impact on life inside the blended family and on the stepmother who is providing the children's daily care.

In her haste to do a good job of parenting, the new stepmother can unwittingly take on far more than she can handle, and push out the very people who should be supporting her. She cannot possibly make up for the trauma of divorce and remarriage just by appearing on the scene and, as we explain in the chapter on the extended family, there are many other people who also have a stake in the children's happiness. First and most important should be the custodial father. Presumably he was managing as a single parent, and he has an obligation to maintain a strong parenting role, no matter how tempting it may be to relax and let a competent, enthusiastic wife take over. It is unfair to transfer the parenting authority solely to the stepmother, and it will not work. Second, of course, is the children's mother. Her support can make the stepmother's task much easier and less involved emotionally with the children. Third, grandparents, aunts, and uncles, relatives of both biological parents, can often provide assistance if they feel it will be accepted. Fourth, are a variety of institutions. Although institutions are very slow in recognizing the special characteristics and needs of stepfamily members, they too have a responsibility to adjust to changes. The more stepmothers decide to ask for support from others in society, the sooner it will come. We know it's more difficult to discuss a stepchild's difficulties with mathematics with his teacher than it would be to have the same discussion about your own child's similar performance, but the more you do it, the easier it becomes.

This may be because stepmothers who take on the challenge of helping raise someone else's children face not only their own expectations that they will do well, but also an awareness that other people are watching to see if they can really manage it.

Adjusting to another set of standards with the other half of a new family takes time. If both partners have children, and it is economically practical, moving into a new home helps to start things off on an even basis. This ensures that no one is moved out of her favorite room or has to share it with a stepsister she is not sure she will like; it means also that nobody will be asked to move his bicycle or skis from his spot in the garage to make room for a stepbrother's sports gear. There will be no pre-established rituals about which kitchen shelf holds the juice glasses or problems when a step-parent wants to change the wallpaper. If one part of the new family has regrets at leaving their former home, so will the others, and the excitement of change may overcome the shared sense of loss.

Since this blended family comes complete with memories and familiar ways of doing things, there are bound to be disagreements or clashes from time to time. It takes a while to establish the particular rhythm of a new family, and the process can be painful. Stepmothers wanting everything to be perfect can be hurt when their efforts are rebuffed or their values questioned. One stepmother felt her stepchildren's antagonism so strongly that she began to suffer a repeated nightmare in which all the fine furniture was removed from the livingroom and replaced by rough wooden benches. Mannequins were set in the front window to give the outside world the impression that this was a conventional family enjoying each others' company. In her dream, as she moved to the kitchen she found their new large pine dining table left bare, while in a far corner her husband and stepchildren appeared to be laughing at her as they set up a meal on a small table from which she and her children were obviously excluded.

When stepmothers also have children of their own, they sometimes worry that they are taking time and energy that belong to them and giving it to the stepchildren. In some cases, this also entails a wider sharing of financial resources. Although our experience counselling children in stepfamilies has not shown that the stepmother's children are anxious about such situations, it may be the stepmother herself who feels shortchanged, having to divide her time so many ways in order to make herself available to all the children. If there are constant struggles about discipline or other day-to-day expectations, the stepmother can come to resent even more the time stepchildren take away from her own.

Along with caring for two sets of children, there is a growing likelihood that today's stepmother will also be holding down an outside job. And although expectations are changing, slowly, about family roles and duties,

women are still doing the majority of the household tasks in Canada. Whether or not she also works outside the home, the remarried woman is still taking on the primary responsibility for the success of the stepfamily. The natural mother without custody may feel a sense of loss, but the stepmother can feel trapped and imposed upon, without anyone being concerned about granting her some free time for herself. A cooperative agreement with the natural mother can be a big help. Natural parents often set children's visiting time to suit their own adult schedules. Sometimes these arrangements should be made with the stepmother's needs in mind.

Age may also make a difference in the step-parenting experience. The glow of love that makes a person feel ready to conquer the world is just as heady the second time around. But this time the newlyweds are no longer in their twenties. High hopes and the best of plans get everything off to a good start, but energy levels are not quite as high when one is thirty or forty. While the children may no longer be babies, the family structure is still at the infant stage. It is important to recognize that it will grow at its own pace; everything cannot be accomplished at once.

Concerns about their own health may arise because stepmothers are usually older than first-time mothers. When a stepmother is ill or needs surgery, a situation which would have seemed fairly manageable in the original family may become much more uncomfortable to handle in a stepfamily. A stepchild may not want to admit he depends on his stepmother, but seeing her ill makes him distinctly nervous because some of his security is slipping.

It is this ambivalence that causes teenagers to act the way Dave, a Vancouver 15-year-old, did when his stepmother had minor surgery. When he came home from school and found she had returned from the hospital, he asked how she was feeling then bluntly suggested, "I guess you'll be going right back to your job." What he probably meant was that he hoped everything in the household would quickly go back to normal. But what it sounded like to Anna, his stepmother, was that her pain and her fears about the surgery just did not matter. Another stepmother arranged to go to a friend's home for a few days' convalescence following surgery, rather than go home where she knew she would feel very uncomfortable asking any of her three stepchildren to help out by bringing her meals to her bedroom.

For many women who have chosen to become stepmothers, the realization that they are part of a minority group comes as a bit of a shock. But by masquerading as a natural mother, altering her true identity in order to fit into a society and to be accepted as part of a "normal" family, a stepmother acts like any member of a minority group who is striving to conform. By pretending to be a "real" mother, she hides her pain and her sense of isolation. But she carries around with her a haunting question: "Why do these children not like me?" Accepting society's mandate that she be a surrogate mother, she ends up being everyone's scapegoat.

Working it out

Approximately 47 per cent of second marriages end in divorce. The major reason for this is said to be problems with children from a first marriage, either his or hers. The dynamics of day-to-day life in the stepfamily can make or break a marriage. If they are based on false premises to start with, they are headed for trouble, and coping with regularly recurring conflicts will wear down a stepmother. The more time she has to spend on settling crises, the less time and energy she will have to use the special talents and positive thinking she brought to the marriage. She has to rechannel her energies along more constructive paths, and the best place to begin is with herself. If she can accept the role of responsible adult, helping the children to make the most of themselves, she establishes the emotional distance that is vital for a healthy, continuing stepfamily. She may admit, a little sadly, as did one stepmother of three teenagers, that "Our home has everything but warmth." But it can have stability, freedom from horrendous blowups, and with luck, once the children reach maturity, an understanding and appreciation of what the stepmother has contributed to their lives.

A stepmother, in a committed partnership with a man who has children from a previous relationship may want to consider herself a parent to those children. However, no matter how important that role may be, it does not reflect the person's whole identity. A stepmother must maintain her step-parenting in perspective and avoid over-identifying with the nurturing, traditional female role. Giving up friends, recreational activities, or even a career will only leave her feeling deprived, frustrated and angry, and will backfire.

She is responsible for nurturing her own happiness and satisfaction in other areas of her life in order to deal with the high demands of her new family. That means knowing the limits of what she can provide and asserting her rights in the family, both with her new partner and with the children. She is an additional parent who has to respect the other family members' need for distance, but she is a full fledged person in her own right.

Anne, a Montreal stepmother, puts it this way: "Walking on eggshells or on a tightrope can't even describe accurately how I feel when the children come back home from their summer camp. If I wait for them at home, they let me know I should have welcomed them at the airport. If I go to wait for them there, with their father, they are uncomfortable because their mother may show up, so they ignore me completely and I feel devastated. I decided to make plans to do things with friends on those days. It helps me gather the strength and patience I need to help the children adjust to being back home. I receive them with a special meal, and in great spirits. My husband did not like my solution at first, but now he is happy with the results."

If she knows that transitional times, such as between the two parents' homes, or other visits and home, are more stressful, the stepmother can prepare for them.

Other high tension situations result from the natural parents having to interact—in arranging children's visits, or discussing financial and other matters. Stepmothers often complain that they find it very difficult to defend themselves from real or perceived intrusions by the children's natural mother.

Suggesting that children need contact with their biological mother does not imply that she should have free access to the remarried couple's home. Calling at 6 a.m. or at suppertime is clearly not beneficial to the children, even if they are happy to hear from their mother. Unpredictable visits or cancelled visits all have implications on a stepmother's life.

Divorced fathers often unwittingly continue to cater to the ex-wife's wishes regarding the children, even if it is destructive to the children and the whole new family, perhaps because of guilt or a lingering attachment to their former wife.

Thirty-eight-year-old Mark, a Thunder Bay carpenter, did not want to challenge the boy's mother, Amy, about support payment for the boys. Even though Kevin, 10, and Ben, 12, had lived with him and his second wife, Clare, almost continuously for the last five years, he still sent Amy monthly cheques. When Mark had to take on an extra job three evenings each week to cover expenses, Clare looked after the boys, cancelling her ceramics class. She resented adding this care to her full-time job and housework.

Clare is a good example of what not to do. To appreciate Mark's concern for Amy, who had a problem with alcohol, is one thing. Giving up something she really enjoyed is quite another. She would have become tired and eventually would have directed her anger at her husband or the children.

It might have been wiser to tell him, "I will be happy to stay at home with the boys one evening a week, but I am busy the other two evenings. You will have to make other arrangements." Mark's loyalty to his former wife needed to be challenged, and a fair share of the housework discussed. The boys were becoming old enough to share some of the housework that their father could not manage along with an extra job.

In order to enjoy the positive benefits of being a stepmother, it is essential for her to clarify her different roles. She has to understand and work out her relationship with her husband; she has to understand and work out her relationship with her stepchildren; and, whether or not she is able to work out a comfortable relationship with the children's natural mother, she must try to understand what that relationship involves.

The couple bond

When the children are there from the very first day, it may be hard to remember that a step-parent did not marry a family. She married another person, and because of that relationship became a step-parent. Although this may sound simplistic, it's vital, because even more than in a nuclear family the bond between husband and wife is the key to continuity in a stepfamily. In the original family, if communication breaks down between the couple, the children retain their connection to both parents. In a stepfamily, the child's connection to the step-parent is through the natural parent who brought him or her into the family. So the most constructive approach for a long-term relationship with the children is to let them observe on a day-to-day basis the mature adults who care enough about each other to consult and work things out together for everyone's benefit.

By putting the marriage first, the stepmother establishes a sense of balance, so problems can be viewed from the couple's perspective. It may take a little while for the children of either or both partners to get used to it, but it also gives them something solid if they are wondering about the stability of the new family. The strength of the marital bond will be the best basis for integrating all the other family members. It establishes immediately the adult-parent partnership and allows all the children to be children rather than their dad or mother's dependable helper.

It's important to know before the marriage whether the father is looking for a wife or a housekeeper. If it's the latter, trying to make the adult relationship the pivot for the stepfamily will be an impossible task. He may want to continue his familiar patterns with his own children while the stepmother carries on in her own way with her children, side by side under the same roof, playing at being a family and wondering when the rewards and satisfactions are going to arrive.

It may seem perfectly normal if her order of priorities goes something like this: first her children, then her spouse, then his children; and his order of priorities goes something like this: his children, her, her children. But in order to build a strong family unit, an adjustment has to be attempted. When the adults put each other at the top of their priority lists, and even if they continue to place their own children before their stepchildren, there is a better chance of avoiding conflicts and establishing a comfortable pattern of daily living. The children will know that their own natural parent is not lost to them, and by placing the spouse at the top of the wife's list she is narrowing the gap between her own children and the stepchildren.

The adjustment will take time. Children who have been living with a single parent will be used to doing many things together as a mother/child or father/child unit. It will feel unnatural at first to be back in a family where there are adult/child boundaries. In one family, teenagers who were in the habit of phoning their father at work every day to discuss what he should buy for supper on the way home were surprised to learn that this bothered their stepmother. For her part, she was refraining from calling her new husband during the day just to say hello because she thought a call from each of his children would already seriously interrupt his work day.

Once the topic came out in the open, he was able to say that he was happy to hear from all of them and that if he was busy he would tell them.

There will be some major reorganizational hurdles when two families try to develop a new pattern of living. A strong regard for each other will help a couple surmount them without trying to compete for dominance in the household. Talking things through and listening to all the family members is time-consuming but absolutely necessary, because a new step-parent coming into the household cannot simply fit into a slot vacated by a former partner who continues to be the children's parent.

Because so many stepmothers come complete with boundless enthusiasm and unrealistic expectations of themselves, it is not surprising that their husbands hope they will have magic solutions for making everything better without any hassles. On the other hand, potential stepmothers are often attracted to men who are looking after their own children because they appear so responsible, capable and caring. If he has a secret hope to hand it all over when he remarries, they may both be in for a shock. Although changes are coming gradually, the women's traditional role of caring for home and family is still the norm in North America. If the couple faces some of these questions together before marriage, and recognize what they are expecting of themselves and each other, the partnership has a better chance of surviving.

Getting along with the children

First of all, stepmothers cannot take the place of mothers. Since most remarriages involve divorced rather than widowed persons, chances are the children's mother is still a part of their lives, whether they live with her, see her often, or worry because they rarely see her. Children of divorced parents can experience a deep sense of loss, but they are not orphans. A stepmother is an extra person coming into their lives. It will take time for them to get to know her.

Sometimes the unresolved anger felt by the children's natural mother following the dissolution of the first marriage is a factor in the children's adjustment to the arrival of a stepmother. They may unwittingly project their mother's emotions against her. Or, if their own mother is unable to show them the affection and support they need, they may express their sadness in the form of hostility toward the stepmother. It's important to remember that the children will almost always love their own mother best and any attempt to compete for the children's affection is asking for trouble.

One stepmother, who left her own job to help her new husband care for his son and tend his farm, was stunned after 10 years of hard work to hear her 13-year-old stepson repeat his natural mother's comments on her actions. The teenager, just home from a visit with his mother, objected to his stepmother's plans for additions to a farm building, pointing out unnecessarily that he was to inherit the farm, not her or her own three children who lived with them.

If a stepmother has not come to expect effusive appreciation for her efforts, and if she is prepared to see many of her offers of help rebuffed, she will not interpret such behavior as a personal attack. Often divided loyalties between the natural mother and the stepfamily make it impossible for a stepchild to relax sufficiently to feel free to enjoy the good things that can come with a stable home. Although deep down they may know it is in their best interest to have the marriage endure, from time to time there are still provocations that seem to be aimed at splitting up the remarried couple. Many children retain for many years, and even into adulthood, the hope that their natural parents will be reunited, irrespective of any evidence to the contrary.

Occasionally, children will provoke dissension between a natural parent and a step-parent to regain their parents' attention. One 10-year-old found this was a great ploy. Every time she had an argument with her stepmother, her father would sit down with her alone for an hour's chat. That response made it even more worthwhile to increase the number of run-ins with the stepmother.

There can also be special problems with the children because they have been hurt by their parents' distress during and after the divorce. Aggressive behavior and unrestrained anger, as well as regression may cause concern. But this should be a shared concern. It is inappropriate for a stepmother to accept the responsibility. It belongs primarily to the parents, and she, as the natural parent's ally, can lend support in helping them find a solution.

As awareness grows of the need to be a responsible adult guiding stepchildren, rather than a replacement mother, the opportunities to enjoy life together will expand. In April, 1983, Ann Landers reproduced for millions of readers a letter sent by a stepmother. Landers commented that she had never printed one like it before, and the fact that it was written at all indicates that there are advances in the way step-parents see their role. The letter read:

"A while back I found myself nodding in agreement when I read these lines in your column: 'The major reason second marriages fail is because of trouble over children from a first marriage—his or hers.' May I say a word, please, to children whose parents have split and who find themselves with a step-parent they resent a little—or a lot?

Dear Children: Since your dad and I married, I have worked right along with him so he could keep up the child-support payments. The flights you make to visit us for holiday and summer vacations are half paid for by me. I share in the bills for your medical and dental care. I buy most of the clothes you wear. I do this willingly because I love your father and recognize that he has an obligation to you, which I am happy to share. When I say 'No' to you, it is because I want you to turn out to be a person of good character who will be able to handle whatever life sends your way. It would be a lot easier to say 'Yes.' No hassle, no arguments, just closing my eyes and ears and letting you do as you please. But I refuse to do that. Children of divorce have a few added problems, but then so do people who marry a divorced person with kids. Please try to understand where I am coming from. It's hard for me, too. But I am willing to meet you more than halfway. If you come 30 per cent down the road, I'll travel the other 70. I am Your Stepmother."

Natural mother—here to stay

Stepmothers who would prefer that the natural mother stay out of the picture so the stepfamily can be more of a "real" family on its own are not being realistic.

Although a divorce has taken place, the parenting bond survives, and the children's father retains a relationship with his former wife through his loyalty to the children. Sometimes an amicable arrangement for caring for the children through joint or shared custody has already been worked out between the natural parents before the remarriage. A stepmother would be wise to encourage the arrangement to continue. Suzanne, a 30-year-old Winnipeg mother of two little girls, recognizes that they are very attached to their father and he is a good parent. During the divorce proceedings, it was agreed that the girls would spend alternate weeks at each parent's home. For Suzanne, this arrangement is working out beautifully because she enjoys her children when she has them, and she enjoys her week off since it gives her a chance to catch up on her friends and other interests. As far as she is concerned, when and if Steve remarries, the children will carry on in the same pattern, giving both sets of adults time with them and time on their own. The stepmother who joins this family will have a much more clearly defined role as an adjunct to the father, than happens when a couple divorces under an adversarial system which grants custody to only one parent.

If the father has custody, the natural mother may feel shortchanged and bitter. Society is much less tolerant of mothers who walk out of a bad marriage without the children than they are of fathers who do the same, and the natural mother who does not have custody can feel deprived and isolated. This is painful for all concerned because mothers and children need to keep in touch with each other. A natural mother who participates in the parenting is much more likely to appreciate the contributions of the stepmother and to encourage her children to make the most of their opportunities.

A mother who can wish her children a happy time as they set off for a vacation with their father and his new wife is helping them immensely, although it can demand great unselfishness. Maureen, staying behind at the Kingston house while her sons joined her former husband Jim and their stepmother Valerie for a skiing holiday in Quebec, refused to be vindictive. She invited Valerie in to see the boy's rooms, pets and card collections before they set off. This showed the boys that their mom respected Valerie and was prepared to share them with her.

What's in it for you?

There are some very positive things to be said about the step-parenting experience. For most individuals they are closely related to the satisfaction and happiness associated with the marriage. If the marital bond is nurtured by allowing for time away from the children just to be with each other, then the time spent together parenting will be much less of a burden.

For stepmothers who do not have children of their own, step-parenting provides an opportunity to share in the many rewards of observing and participating in the growth of children from stage to stage. Here is a second chance to learn to fly a kite, whistle a tune or go tobogganing. Here is a chance to share in the excitement of a little boy or girl who does well in a race, brings home a report card that shows how hard he or she is trying, or steps onto the stage in a school play. It is difficult not to feel good about contributing to someone's achievements.

Children who have been through the experience of their parent's divorce and remarriage need a chance to act their age in the knowledge that their family supports them. By playing a positive adult role and wishing them the best, a stepmother contributes enormously to their chances of growing up with a strong feeling of self-esteem and self-confidence. Knowing that you can have such an impact on a child's future is a big responsibility, and it is better to share it with the many others who are also concerned with the same child. Marriage into a family with children brings an extended family of relatives who care about them. Some may turn out to be good friends if they are encouraged to continue to be an important part of the children's lives.

A stepmother who brings her own children to a blended family can find that they, too, are enriched by the experience. Of course adjustments have

to be made, but learning to adapt will serve children well throughout their lives. Above all, they will learn that relationships demand commitment and hard work.

As the number of second marriages increase, so do the number of stepfamilies. By taking a truly realistic view of what is involved in being a stepmother, more women will be able to retain their enthusiasm and joie de vivre. As they do, and as they continue to share their experiences with others in the same situation, the benefits and satisfactions of this experience can also increase.

Recommendations

Stepmother

1. Strive for a strong relationship with your spouse.
2. Remember that you are a new member of a new family, not a replacement for an absent member.
3. Don't attempt to be a SuperMom. It doesn't work.

4. Maintain a healthy distance from the children.
5. Make use of the assistance of the extended family, including the natural mother.
6. Maintain interests, friends and activities from your former life.
7. Remember to care for yourself.
8. When you are angry at your husband for not backing you up, don't get angry at the children. It's his responsibility to make sure they treat you with respect.

Custodial father

1. Take a clear stand in support of your present partner, then don't respond to the children's pressures about loyalty.
2. Keep in mind that the children are *your* primary responsibility and that of your ex-wife, with whom you must cooperate even though the marriage is over.
3. Be aware that you may have conflicting feelings about sharing parenting with your new spouse when it means giving up the omnipotent role with the children you had as a single parent.
4. Be sure you are clear whether you want a wife or a housekeeper.

Natural mother

1. Remember that kids can get help from many people, but don't count yourself out. They still need you.
2. Competing for the kids' love will only serve to confuse them. Your strong position is already established and if you can appreciate your continuing role, everyone can share productively in the children's lives.
3. Do your share of the ongoing care, despite what you may feel toward the stepmother.

Children

1. Try to observe and think things out for yourself.
2. Recognize that a stable home is best for you.
3. Everyone in your family should be treated with courtesy. You have a right to dislike or to love anyone who has a claim on your affections, but courtesy toward those with whom you are living is a must.
4. Understand that the divorce was between your parents; they didn't divorce you. But their conflicts have caused problems for you too, and they are the people who should help you work them out.
5. Relationships take time to develop, so get to know people before making decisions about them.

Chapter Two

Taking Care

By the time she was five years old, Amy had begun to fear that her world was falling apart. The parents she loved and depended upon could no longer hide their unhappiness with one another from her. Suddenly she was burdened with anxieties she could not understand.

When her mother complained about the strain of taking care of her, Amy was frightened that she would leave; but when her parents quarreled, Amy was the one her mother looked to for comfort. So the five-year-old tried her best to be a "perfect child," hoping in this way to avert the break-up of her family. Behind the accommodating behavior lurked the tummy-aches and the nightmares—painful expressions of her tremendous anxiety.

Instead of the security the child deserved, she faced adult emotional strains she could not understand, let alone cope with logically. Feeling deprived of love and stability, she had few options. Should she turn to her father? Although she was influenced by her mother into thinking that he was "bad," Amy recalled that he had never threatened to leave her, and that at times he had taken her to the playground or a movie in order to free her from the tensions building up at home. Could she count on her mother who was having such difficulty simply caring for herself—and whose anger and bitterness toward her husband were signals to Amy that she too could become the object of her mother's wrath? Above all, how could Amy continue to believe that she was a lovable little human being whose feelings deserved to be respected?

Of course not every child experiences such a profound sense of fear or loss at the time of parental separation. The age and personality of the child as well as the level of tension or disruption in the home will make a difference in a child's ability to cope with upheaval. But no matter how great or small the impact of the parental split, it will remain a part of that child's experience and must be respected by those who later care for him or her.

The long term effects have not been clearly established, but there is growing concern that children of divorce suffer emotional pain for years.

Julie Autumn List, in her autobiographical account of a daughter's view of her parents' divorce, *The Day the Loving Stopped*, expresses this hurt vividly:

"We, the children, are the victims of our parents' mistakes. Obviously no father or mother willfully hurts their children when they realize they no longer love each other. But the pain which results from the separation and the "regrouping" is inevitable. People say that children are adaptable; they adjust to new environments and make different friends easily. Children, they say, like tennis balls off a wall, bounce back. They struggle to grow up and because they are so resilient, they survive. I agree—children are terrific survivors. What I experienced is nothing compared to the horrors witnessed by children in concentration camps, from alcoholic families, from extremely poor homes, of battered wives, or from foster homes. I was, in no sense of the word, a "deprived" child. Even those children who have truly suffered, who have never known the love I have felt, continue to live and overcome their pasts. The scars are there, however. I believe that we children feel more than we reveal; we hurt more than we are able to cry; and we perceive the truth of what is happening around us most of the time. Children bounce back because we know no other life than this.

"A year ago, my uncle and his wife separated after eight years of marriage and a son, who was about to celebrate his sixth birthday. My only first cousin, beautiful and blond, lovingly spoiled and wise. As I watched their marriage end, even though the circumstances were entirely different, I felt as though I were reliving something too closely. I found that in spite of my love for my aunt and uncle, I could not speak to them as they waged their war over the future of their child. Why couldn't they see what they were doing to him? I wrote in my journal,

January 31, 1978
Another victim. Little boy who knows only that Daddy and Mommy fight, don't live together, fly back and forth across the country, depositing him. Happy birthday little cousin. Six years old and already so confused. The process will begin—the pain, the exchange of visits, holidays, two birthdays, two Christmases, the double life. Nothing will ever be normal again—the break, the splintering, the turning point. How I wish I could save you from the hurt you will know, the loss you will feel. The loss of the family; no, the <u>death</u> of the family. The beginning of the new life, the strange and unfamiliar pattern of <u>Mommy</u> or Daddy—Mommy with other men, Daddy with other women. There's no road back to normalcy, ever... We <u>are</u> the passed-around generation... <u>Let me never make a victim of a child of mine...</u>"

Statistics Canada figures tell us that each year 65,000 Canadian children experience the divorce of their parents. Predictions are that by 1990, fully one-third of the children in this country will be affected by parental divorce before they reach the age of 18. A minority of these children will experience few lasting repercussions from the change in their lives. A majority, however, will experience varying degrees of distress, disruption and pain that may remain with them into adulthood. A stepmother entering these children's lives will find her task more or less difficult depending upon whether or not a child received needed support at the time of the divorce to allow him or her to adjust to changed circumstances. The presence or absence of such caring support will have influenced the child's behavior and readiness to cope with further change when a parent remarries.

In this chapter, we look at some aspect of caring on a day-to-day basis for the child's physical and emotional well-being. And, as in all areas we discuss, this responsibility is not the stepmother's alone. She is only one member of the team.

However, the stepmother has a definite role to play. A woman who marries a man with children is committing herself to being a responsible adult in the lives of those children. Her responsibilities and opportunities may differ from those of the natural parents, but irrespective of the children's age, she represents a new adult in their lives.

It's not easy to care for stepchildren. How can a stepmother measure how well she is doing? Even natural parents often have doubts when raising their own children, so it should come as no surprise that the stepmother is concerned, especially since the children may well have had some confusion in their lives already. Success in such a case cannot be measured in terms of a child's love for the stepmother or lack of it, but she should, for example, make it a point to follow his/her progress in school and socially. Being a part of their successes can bring her a sense of satisfaction, even though the children may not respond to her help with any obvious signs of acceptance or appreciation. Expressions of approval and the encouragement to persist will come more appropriately from the children's natural father, as well as from other members of the children's extended family, including their grandparents, who are in a position to acknowledge the stepmother's efforts on the children's behalf.

Taking care of children begins with an awareness of their needs, along with a realistic assessment of what can be done. It will not always be possible to respond to every need, either because of financial constraints or limits of physical energy. It is not possible to erase the things that have already happened in a child's life, and some of these experiences will pose problems in terms of providing appropriate care. Knowing that it is not always within a stepmother's power to fulfill all the children's needs, and understanding what things cannot be changed, will allow her to feel less hurt when all does not go smoothly. Unrealistic expectations of oneself or the children can only increase her vulnerability to hurt and anger. In this chapter we attempt to provide a realistic picture of the opportunities available to stepmothers caring for stepchildren, the most important consideration to keep in mind being that she is an *additional* adult in their lives.

Points to consider:

First of all, many children negatively affected by divorce will enter a stepfamily with a number of unresolved issues and behavior patterns that will take some time to work out. Some may never be worked out. Others may be short-term problems that need immediate attention, while still others may require a long-term effort or the help of a mental-health professional. Children's reactions to their parents' divorce and remarriage differ greatly, but their developmental stages provide some clues.

Secondly, the cooperation and continuity in parenting by both natural parents is crucial for the child's adjustment, not only during the divorce, but through the single parenting stage and on into the stepfamily. A lack of continuity with either parent can be detrimental to the child.

Third, a child's receptiveness to a stranger, especially a new person in his/her father's life, will be strongly influenced by how he/she has been affected by the original family break-up and by how much time and attention each of the natural parents have provided the child.

Fourth, it is the responsibility of both natural parents to help the children accept the reality of the remarriage and the fact that the stepmother will be included in a system of shared parenting. The custodial parent, in this case the father, must recognize that the ongoing parental involvement of the children's natural mother is, in most cases, essential for their emotional growth and development. Moreover, the mother's attitude toward the remarriage, and particularly toward the stepmother who will be providing some of the care for her children, will make a big difference in the children's ability to accept the new person in their lives.

Fifth, the new stepmother must realize that the care she is providing the children is a supplement to that provided by the two natural parents. Her role is not to try to take anyone's place—and certainly not that of the natural mother.

We shall examine each of these points because they allow us to set the scene and to consider the practical possibilities in caring for the children.

The effects of divorce and remarriage on children

Successful parenting requires an understanding of the developmental stages of the children, and the subsequent setting of realistic expectations. When parenting children of divorce, however, it is necessary to keep in mind that the rate at which they move through stages will probably be affected by their experience. Some may have suffered varying degrees of emotional upset, making it difficult for them to relate to others. Along with the predictable hesitation and apprehension that can accompany the arrival of a new person in any family, a stepmother may find that the confusion the child has already experienced makes her task more complex.

Most studies of children of divorce have focused on those who continued to live with their mother. We suspect, based on our professional experience, that children who remain with their fathers suffer more, primarily because of the loss of daily contact with the natural mother. Although courts are gradually granting more fathers custody of their children, or encouraging joint parenting, until recently fathers who were caring for their children on their own were doing so largely because the mothers could not.

Researchers are now also finding that the effects of divorce last much longer than originally believed. Recent literature indicates that the child's age at the time of the parents' divorce is not as critical as the support the child receives to help cope with the change. Those who just had to "tough it out," unaided, run a higher risk of subsequently requiring counselling for academic problems, aggressive behavior or abuse of drugs and alcohol.

Nicholas Zill, Ph.D., senior staff scientist with the Foundation for Child Development, Boston, says that divorce significantly increases children's risk of emotional and behavioral problems, and that they are twice as likely to need psychiatric help than children from families that remain intact. S. Jalal Shamsie, child psychiatrist and director of research and education at Thistletown Regional Centre, Rexdale, Ont., noted in a summary of the literature that all children, regardless of age, showed *some* effects of their parents' divorce five years after the event; that one-third of those in a large study were still troubled and distressed five years later; and, that a similar proportion were aware of continuing bitterness between their parents. The literature also indicates an increase in anti-social behavior, depression, and a tendency to run away or attempt suicide, among children from divorced families.

Children who do not feel good about themselves manifest their unhappiness in many disruptive ways. Stepmothers seeking professional help report various behavioral difficulties in their stepchildren, such as unpleasant eating habits, ranging from excessive amounts and hoarding to blatantly rejecting the stepmother's cooking. Other behavioral problems negatively affecting the family atmosphere include poor personal hygiene, stealing, and rudeness toward both the stepmother and the natural father. If stepmothers understood the source of these types of behavior, they would be better prepared to deal with them. Rather than see them as personal affronts or attacks, they would recognize them for what they are: manifestations of unresolved tensions that were present before a stepmother entered the picture.

It is not our purpose here to review all the mental health literature on the effects of divorce since we are addressing the "normal" adjustments required in new families. However, it is important to note that some children do need special, professional care, and recognizing when counselling may be indicated will influence a stepmother's chance of successfully caring for her husband's children.

When a custodial parent remarries, the children experience an additional sense of loss. It signals clearly what they do not want to believe—that the original family will not be re-established. It also means the custodial parent will now be focusing a good deal of his attention on his adult partner, and therefore spending less time with the children. If the step-parent also brings children to the new household, an additional adjustment period will follow where the children jostle for position and struggle for stability.

Of course, a child's needs at various ages will determine the support he/she requires at that time. During infancy and pre-school years, children require the most physical care and rely most heavily on their parents. As they grow older, physical needs diminish, but emotional needs remain. Bonnie Robson, M.D., of the C.M. Hincks Treatment Centre in Toronto, outlines the effects in terms of the developmental stage of the child at the time of divorce. She says that by being aware of the developmental stages, parents are most likely to give the child the immediate assistance needed to cope. Although babies under two years of age have been found to be more ready than older children to accept a parent's new partner as a substitute for a natural parent, those over two may experience intense anxiety at separation from a parent. They recall infancy as a safe time when they were loved and protected, and some regress to babyish behavior. From birth to five years of age, children need consistent predictable routines and dependable parenting from one or two primary caregivers. Three to five-year-olds also need explanations about what's happening when there are changes.

Four-year-old Linda, who had been almost three when her parents separated, would not leave her father's side when he had friends over to the apartment. When Karen, 24, began to come visiting more frequently, Linda also began to cling to her. The two adults were rarely alone since Linda was always sticking to one or the other. When they picked her up at nursery school, she would complain about her bad experiences there with a "you shouldn't leave me" tone in her voice. Gradually, as her Dad and Karen, who later became her stepmother, allowed her time to be close to them, she became more at ease and able to play on her own without the constant need for physical reassurance.

Linda had experienced the same reality as five-year-old Amy. Sometimes, in the adult turmoil of separation, explaining to the children what is happening may be the most difficult thing for parents to do calmly and reassuringly. While children need the most physical care during this early childhood phase, a stepmother may find on joining the family that they want many things done but do not want her to do them. It is difficult for young children to accept help or closeness from a new person until they have begun to trust her. So a new stepmother can be most helpful by not trying too hard; rather she should encourage the father in his parenting and remind him that the children need lots of hugs and affection from the time he gets home each day until bedtime.

Children in the early school years (six to eight), will also feel more comfortable with a little distance in the relationship with the step-parent. Very anxious to keep up ties with the non-custodial parent, they are not in a rush to sit on a stepmother's lap. Dr. Robson notes that this is the age group that feels most responsible for the parents' separation, and is most vulnerable to hurt. The children tend to protect themselves from anxiety by using denial and a sense of wishful thinking. But they can also feel a great deal of guilt, hoping that if they are good their parents will get back together. A child of this age is deeply affected by any hostility shown by one parent toward the other. It is vitally important that the child be told the reasons for his parents' separation in order to understand the difference between the ongoing parental bond affecting him, and the marital tie between his parents, which has come to an end. Frequent phone calls, visits and easy access to both parents must be arranged. A child of this age group needs to be allowed to express his feelings. He is also helped by knowing there is a clear custody decision and he can count on some consistent daily pattern.

Nine-to-12-year olds have fewer physical needs, but their emotional needs still must be met. Dr. Robson believes they can benefit from talking with a neutral adult at the time of the family separation. This age group usually holds strongly to the principle of fair play and does not want to be drawn into a parental blaming game. Exposed to propaganda by one or both sides, the child may solve the conflict about loyalty to both by overdepending on one parent and totally rejecting the other. By being helped to see both sides, and encouraged to maintain contact with both parents, there is a greater chance of his adjusting to the single-parent household and, later, to a possible remarriage of either or both parents. Otherwise, the anger that had been directed at the absent parent can be displaced onto the new marital partner and severely disrupt the development of the blended family.

Anger is one of the most prevalant effects seen in children of divorce and, particularly with boys, it seems to increase following a parent's remarriage, regardless of who the new step-parent is or what he or she is like. One nine-year-old who had known his new stepmother for years, and had loved her as a babysitter between the time he was two and five, became very upset when his father married her. Strange as it may seem, it is much easier to express hostility than to reveal sadness, disappointment or love. Displaying anger is a safer, less personal and less threatening behavior for a child than expressing tenderness, affection, fear or anxiety. That may not be fair to the stepmother, but recognizing a child's difficulty in developing a close relationship can cause a stepmother to lower her expectations and provide the child with the protective distance he needs. The angry feelings that well up spontaneously when a stepmother feels rejected or unappreciated can be shared with other adults, not taken out on the child.

Other feelings of children of divorce that can influence their adjustment to a stepfamily situation include self-blame and a fear of abandonment, along with hopes for reunification of the original family. Often left in the dark about the basis for custody decisions, children sometimes decide on their own that the good parent lost out. They view the parent with whom they live as the bad parent because he/she also happens to be the disciplinarian setting the day-to-day rules. That parent's new partner and ally will also be branded a "bad parent," so children who have these feelings will find it difficult to accept a step-parent. Natural resistance to an outsider will be augmented by a sense of disloyalty to the "good parent" who is absent if the child makes any welcoming gesture toward the stepmother.

Some children's expectations of their stepmother can be based on confused memories of the original family leading them to reproach the stepmother for not measuring up to a fantasy. Hugh, at 13, expected that when his father remarried the family would operate the way he recalled it as a child. He remembered his mother awaiting him at noon with a hot lunch. However, that was in his first three years of primary school. He had forgotten that during the next three years he went to the neighbor's house for lunch since his mother was at work. In grades seven and eight, he packed his own lunch and took it to school. By this time, his mother had left the family and his father cared for him and his brothers. With his father's remarriage, he somehow expected that everything would revert to those early, precious days when hot lunch was ready on the table. His stepmother, now caring for a family of five teenagers, plus her own full-time job, was willing to pack school lunches, but she found it very painful to be viewed as the mean stepmother just because she could not provide a condition that had not been a part of Hugh's life for at least five years.

When children are in their teens at the time of divorce, parental separation can intensify adolescent rebellion since the event itself hastens the end of the period of heavy parental dependency. Teenagers can experience intense loyalty conflicts, and at the same time feel angry at a parent who appears to be undermining or blaming the other for the situation. Although parents may feel sad when their teenagers look outside the family for support and understanding, they must keep in mind that this is a natural reaction at this stage, one which provides teenagers with an opportunity to get away from family dissension. Above all else, what they need from their parents is discipline and consistent expectations, although they can seldom admit it, even to themselves.

There are some who need special understanding and care. A child who had to take on responsibilities early in life may appreciate a chance to regress for a time. Anna was 17 when her father remarried a woman with three boys, leaving her as the eldest in a family of five children. She appeared to adjust well to the daily routine, got along cordially with her stepmother, while keeping in close touch with her natural mother, for whom she felt somewhat protective. Her own need of nurturing and protection was demonstrated in her bedroom, which she decorated herself. Although the wallpaper and furnishings were more feminine than childish, her bed was adorned with a dozen dolls and teddy bears, most showing signs of plenty of hugging. Not until she was 23, and ready to share an apartment with several friends, did she make any changes to that comforting environment—her one way of remaining a little girl for a few years longer than the other children needed to.

Working out a personal value system is an important task of the adolescent years. This can be difficult for a teenager whose parents are divorced and have conflicting opinions and values. By supporting an opinion, or choosing a fashion that one parent recommends, a teen may fear that this will be interpreted as a rejection of the other parent's choices, and therefore a rejection of him or her. As she grows older, a teenager has to learn to stand by his/her decisions in terms of how they affect him/her, rather than in terms of whose side he/she appears to support. A stepmother, who adopts the role of a mature, neutral adult, can be an important ally as she quietly supports a teenager's moves toward independent thinking.

Having spoken of the long-lasting effects of divorce on children—many of them negative and painful—we must also acknowledge that some children are positively affected by their parents' divorce. One study of college students found that stepchildren who had gone through the experience of their parents' divorce could not be distinguished from the students from intact families. Children of stepfamilies have also been found to have a strong sense of responsibility and to be more conscious of the power of destructive relationships and the joy of healthy ones.

Continuing and cooperative parenting

Divorce has become more commonplace, but society is only beginning to recognize that co-parenting continues as a long-term responsibility. It can go on for many years. Young people in their twenties are often still either living with a parent or returning home at regular intervals. Difficult as it may be to establish a cordial, fair and constructive pattern of working things out together, the divorcing couple must consider first and foremost the welfare of young children who are not in a position to make the best arrangements for themselves.

Numerous studies have shown that when the adults put their own needs and emotions aside to ensure that their children have set times to see each parent, the children's self-esteem is helped immensely. A child who is aware of both his mom and dad's concern is going to consider himself worthy of being concerned about. Hearing that familiar voice on the phone, or seeing the familiar face on a regular, predictable basis go a long way toward reassuring a child that the transition will be fine after all, and that the future holds some promise. Ongoing parenting by both mother and father comes first. The cooperative part can take some time to work out, and guidelines can help.

It stands to reason that the more self-confidence a child has, the more readily he will accept a new adult in his mother's or father's life. Every child will be affected to some degree by a divorce, but the care with which changes are made in his life will determine just how disturbing they really are. Remaining in the same neighborhood, going to the same school, and retaining friends, may all be very important, but most important is ensuring that the child can reach both parents as often as necessary. On the other hand, a child who has no contact or hears only negative things about the absent parent will worry if for any reason that parent is unavailable to him. Children need both parents to provide for their physical and emotional needs.

Other people, including step-parents, will inevitably play a smaller role, at least initially. But a new person in the home will not seem threatening as long as the two natural parents are actively involved in the child's life. A child will understand clearly that the stepmother is not taking the mother's place. Father's new partner will take some getting used to, but if the the co-parenting has been reliable, the anxiety attributable to this further development will be minimized.

A stepmother who finds ongoing negotiations between her husband and his ex-wife on matters concerning the children somewhat disturbing should keep in mind that it is to the new marriage's benefit to have mutual agreement on matters of visits and sharing the children's time. If a non-custodial mother is living far away or rejects her parental responsibilties, the children's unhappiness will have repercussions on the new family. However, in working out schedules for visiting or living with one or the other parent, the stepmother has a right to expect her schedule to be taken into account also.

The response to the step-parent

Remarriage is another shock to children who have seen their first family break down and are wondering what a second family will be like. No matter how well personalities might otherwise blend, one of the most important factors is that the stepmother has now become the father's wife. For some children, that in itself may be the only thing they have against her. Adult children often feel some uneasiness also, but stepmothers usually do not have to get along with them on a daily basis. One 38-year-old woman told of her father remarrying following her mother's long illness and death. Even though she admired her father's new wife, and was able to tell her children that she was happy to see their grandfather content again, she admitted to some resentment. She summed it up with the feeling, "but she's not my mother." Although she knew she was being irrational, it was a strong feeling. For young children facing a new stepmother, the feeling can be much stronger.

Often a stepmother is caught in a double bind where the children need assistance but will not accept hers. Children who miss the warm, nurturing relationship with a natural parent will not be satisfied with someone else's overtures. One stepmother spontaneously resting her hand on her teenage stepson's shoulder as he sat at the supper table immediately felt him pulling away, and realized that a year in the same household had not earned her that privilege yet. Some children have developed a special attachment to their father while he was caring for them without a partner. It will take time and understanding on the part of the couple to help the child realize that he or she is still loved and valued even though the adults have their own special bond.

Often there are no clues to help a stepmother figure out how well or how badly she is doing. This requires mutuality, where both persons want to reach out at the same time because of a need to work out some harmony and equilibrium in the relationship or situation. In stepfamilies, however, children can display a strong resistance to reaching any kind of equilibrium within a household they have not yet completely accepted. Such children may develop an uncanny ability to mask any clues that can give a stepmother an idea of where she is going right or wrong. Until she can get to know the children better, for example, she will not be able to tell whether the children hate the supper she cooked because it's different from the way their mother did it, or because it's too much the same.

Part of the stepmother's caring is to respect the special needs of children who have experienced the loss of their original family and are struggling to come to terms with their new reality. The stepmother's task is often difficult so she must keep in mind that, being human, she will have some failures as well as successes.

The reality of the remarriage

How well a new stepmother fits into the picture will depend a good deal on the natural father's willingness to see her as a partner, and on the parenting arrangements he has been able to work out with his former wife. If he can negotiate a plan the adults feel comfortable with, they can cooperate to help the children accept the new situation rather than introducing further confusion.

Trying to coordinate child care with a natural mother is not always easy, especially if she is hostile and the children are aware of it. Not much has been written about single fathers or the effects of their remarriage on the natural mothers, but this event can certainly reactivate feelings of loss and pain. Sometimes in her anger, jealousy, or distress, the natural mother may further withdraw from the children, avoiding commitments and skipping promised visits. It is not uncommon for the natural mother to feel threatened by the fact that another woman is competently looking after her children.

Unfortunately for most stepfamilies, there is still no established, acceptable way to routinely include the outside parent in the care of the children. This can lead to poor communication and a tug-of-war situation over the children. Guidelines to protect children from this feeling of being yanked in both directions are set out in *Mom's house/Dad's house*, by Ricci (Macmillan, 1980). The author suggests a New Family Bill of Rights, which includes six points.

1. Each child has the right to an independent and meaningful relationship with each parent.
2. Each child has the right to be free from listening to, or being part of, parents' personal battles. Neither parent uses the child as a go-between or uses the time spent with the other parent as a threat or bargaining chip.
3. Each parent has the right and responsibility to contribute to the raising of his or her child.
4. Each parent has the right, during time spent with the children, to follow his or her own standards, beliefs or style of child-raising without unreasonable interference from the other parent.
5. Each parent has the right to his or her own private life and territory.

6. Each parent and child have the right to call themselves families, no matter how the children's time is divided.

Guidelines like these might help avoid situations such as the following described by a Toronto stepmother. She was so upset when her stepson returned from visiting his mother bearing a container of his favorite chocolate syrup, that without thinking of his feelings, she yanked the syrup from his hands and poured it down the kitchen sink, yelling that she could make the same stuff and did not need any help in this. She was reacting to the fact that his mother had been of no help when the eight-year-old had recently been sick. At the time, a simple phone call would have helped to reassure him and would have been appreciated by his stepmother who was helping him through sleepless nights. Irrespective of the stepmother's reasons for her anger, however, it was not the little boy's fault that he was caught in the middle. His mother may have made the syrup because she loved him and wanted him to have something from her house, or indeed, she may have been competing with the stepmother. Either way, the child's feelings should have been protected rather than assaulted by the stepmother's anger, no matter how much self-restraint it demanded of her. It's not always easy!

Expecting the two women to become friends is usually asking too much—although it does happen on occasion. Much more common is an admission of shared responsibility, with no other interaction. Establishing at least this type of working arrangement provides insurance for those times when everyone is concerned over a particular problem or event, such as illness or hospitalization of a child, arrangements for various types of ceremonies, and so on. Illness can be alarming for all parents, and arrangements made by the stepmother are sometimes changed by the natural mother, leading to a measure of frustration. However, a child's place is not in the middle of an adult wrangle, particularly if he is sick. He is not responsible for the problem, so the stepmother must again remain calm and sensible and possibly take a back seat to make sure the child's life is not complicated by several decision makers.

Children with behavioral difficulties, learning disabilities or other problems require extra care from the stepmother. If possible, she must also establish smooth, ongoing contacts with the natural mother to help share the additional support necessary, including such matters such as appointments with professional helpers.

If the natural mother has been in the habit of suddenly cancelling arrangements with the children, or expecting their father to take them for a weekend on short notice, a stepmother's request for some predictability in planning may come as a surprise; but it's a valid request. If the father makes arrangements with the children's mother without consulting his new wife, he is denying her role as an important person in his life and ignoring her need for consideration. The father who has custody of the children faces a major task in incorporating his new marital status into his parenting routine. But as the pivotal parent, the one on whom the children are depending most, he is in the best position to ask for the help he needs. Another positive step he can take for everyone's benefit is to reach out to other members of the extended family to support the children within the remarriage.

The Stepmother's caring

Is it my job now to do the laundry for seven? Am I completely responsible for keeping the household in order? Are they expecting their dirty clothes to be collected from their rooms and their clean, folded laundry delivered? If I don't make the dentist appointments, who will? Who checks to make sure their homework is completed?

No matter how well or how badly parents have worked out arrangements for taking care of their children, the stepmother is not coming into the family to take over. The children are not orphans, and the stepmother is just one among several meaningful adults in their lives. Although most of us have not known the extended family involvement of a few generations ago, or of some Asian and African cultures, extra adults sharing a concern for children is not an unusual phenomenon. It need not diminish parental authority, nor infringe on a parent's role. A stepmother has a unique opportunity to be one of those extra caring influences on a child's life.

Her presence alone can set an example of cooperative, healthy living for the children. Children who have witnessed noisy, tumultuous scenes or periods of grim silence in their previous families can benefit greatly from observing and relating to a woman who is getting along with their Dad. It can be a corrective emotional experience.

Sometimes children, especially teenagers, wonder if they are extra baggage now that their father has chosen a new wife; they seek the reassurance that their home is still available to them. Feeling like a fifth wheel, they may turn down offers to accompany the couple to a movie or restaurant. Beneath the teenager's apparent independence may lie a genuine desire to be included, mixed with a feeling that he should not burden the new marriage with his presence.

The stepmother who attempts to establish her place within the household by insisting on recreating the original family model will find that only serves to increase the children's hostility and anxiety. If she can be more realistic, acknowledge that she is not and cannot replace their mother, but is prepared to take an active leadership role with their father in this different kind of family, the children can relax a little.

Successful stepmothers define early what it is they can do for the children, what they want to do, and what they are definitely not going to do. It's helpful to tell them directly what you mean:

"I will mend any of your clothes that need mending—if you will put what needs to be done on the table in the hallway. I won't look around for them."

"I'll make the supper and it will be ready at 6:30 for the family. If you arrive home late, you are welcome to help yourself to your own supper and clean up afterwards, but I won't be serving it."

"I'm available. If you want to talk, I'll listen. If you've had a fight with your brother and you want to tell me about it, I'll be here."

Depending on the stage in the child's life, a stepmother will also often feel responsible for seeing that he or she has a well-rounded schedule. If that means making sure there are drives available for sporting or other activities, it becomes part of the caring. At another stage, for example, when a teenager turns laundry into an issue by using and tossing into the hamper several towels a day, caring means keeping this behavior in perspective. Many adolescents, not just stepchildren, have no awareness about who is washing those towels. Don't take it personally. Teach him how to use the washing machine.

Establishing bedtimes to ensure that children get their required rest is the responsibility of the adults in the house. But when the children visit the non-custodial parent, they abide by the rules of that house. However, school attendance is not a matter of choice. If the non-custodial parent does not follow the same schedule as in the custodial parent's home, it is up to the natural parents to work it out together.

A reality of the 1980s is that a majority of mothers, including stepmothers, work outside the home, either full or part-time. Children will not automatically understand what this represents in terms of the demands it places on their stepmother's energy and time. They need to be helped to understand.

Placing expectations and value on the children's participation in the smooth running of the household also provides a boost to their self-esteem. When deciding what duties she will take on, a stepmother would be wise to find out if the children really want her to be doing some of these things. Maybe getting up at six a.m. to give a child breakfast before swimming practice will be seen by that child as interference in the time she usually gets to talk privately with her Dad. Not every child wants to be greeted with milk and cookies every day after school. Doing too much can backfire, as a stepmother can begin to resent the extra duties. On the other hand, the withdrawal of services, once started, can be seen as depriving the children.

Children's needs can differ from day to day. There are times when it's vitally necessary for them to be able to tell the neighborhood bully, "Here's my mother, back from the grocery store, so you better leave me alone." Then there are other days when they would rather think of you as a friend than a mother. This can be enhanced if there are opportunities to spend time with the children when their father is away so they can see you as an individual in your own right.

The physical care of children comes first, because it cannot wait, and because they will allow it long before any emotional closeness. However, doing the laundry, making the doctor's appointments, driving the children to ballet, hockey or music lessons, and getting them off to bed at a decent hour can become very tedious in the absence of emotional attachment. But

pressing for emotional closeness before children are ready for it (and some may never be ready for closeness with a stepmother), can lead more to anger and an unwillingness to cooperate than maintaining a friendly distance. Getting to know the children and developing an understanding of developmental stages will be much more productive than assuming that warm family feelings spontaneously sprout just because people are all living under one roof.

Although a stepmother knows, as a rule, that her actions cannot compensate a child who wants her mother, there are times when it is vital to take on extra duties. When Dorothy's mother said she could not handle her on a visit if she had the "flu," Jane found herself offering to stay home from a weekend camping trip to care for her six-year-old stepdaughter.

She felt very comfortable caring for her, and reading her stories and knowing she would have not enjoyed her camping trip under the circumstances. However, a few years later when Dorothy was 13 and her mother's promise to take her to a special concert fell through, Jane did not volunteer to rescue the situation because she knew that Dorothy was capable of dealing with the broken promise on her own.

Though it may take some getting used to, in many ways a stepmother who stands back a little can be more effective in creating happy situations for the children and a caring support system with which they are comfortable. She may not be the person they turn to in distress or great happiness, but by making sure that they have opportunities to see their natural mother often, to participate in gatherings with members of their original family, and to feel at ease making friends and inviting them to their home, the stepmother is going a long way towards ensuring the children's well-being. Monitoring a child's progress in school, his competence in extra-curricular programs, or his interest in socializing with others of his own age can give a stepmother a sense of how things are going, and when they are going well, she can take part of the credit.

A critical factor in a stepmother's care for stepchildren is maintaining a positive attitude towards visits to the natural parent or shared time.

Keeping track of bus, train or plane schedules, and accommodating the household schedule to make sure they can come and go on time is caring. Whether this is every other weekend, or several times a month, or only summers and Christmas, the transition from one home to the other must be carried out as smoothy as is humanly possible. This can sometimes prove complicated. It is more easily accomplished in some families or at some times than others, but taking the trauma out of the visits can go a long way to helping a child develop happily. Although not completely within the stepmother's and custodial father's power, a constructive attitude to maintaining contact with the natural mother will also help the child. For everyone's sake, including their own, stepmothers must encourage or at least tolerate these visits without trying to sabotage the arrangements. Feeling jealous of the natural mother who has a bond, through the children, with the man who is now your husband will not help the present or the future. The original parenting is now history, and the stepmother can damage her own marriage by negative actions or attitudes towards the natural mother.

Taking care of stepchildren is a challenge, a long-term one. By understanding the effects of their parents' divorce on their lives, seeking the cooperation of their natural parents, and encouraging other members of their extended family—the aunts, uncles, grandparents—to keep in touch with the children, a stepmother can help to ensure that much of the emotional nurturing is assumed by those who have a biological bond. A child who feels loved by so many people will more easily adapt to the realities of life in a new family and participation in the daily schedule of expectations and commitments.

Suggestions

For stepmothers

You did accept a certain responsibility for the children when you married their father. In addition to stepping into the stepmother role, you are a new person for the kids to relate to. You'll have to decide how much you can give them, and how much you are willing to give up to provide a home for them.

Can you appreciate their dilemma in accepting you, rather than expect instant rewards for your input? Your ability to do so will partly decide how you will get along.

Recognize that you will not be the most important person in their lives, but that you can be a significant influence from whom they can learn. How much they benefit will depend on the children's ability to go beyond an exclusive alliance with their biological mother. At first, the stepchildren, like you, will probably be uncomfortable with the new family. But you are the adult, and you can lead the way as much as they let you. Ideally you may be able to adopt a cooperative plan with their natural mother.

For natural mothers

Be aware that your ex-husband's new wife does not have primary responsibility for your children. If you truly care about your children, you should be grateful for, and support, the efforts the stepmother makes for them.

It may be painful to see someone else at your ex-husband's side, but don't take these feelings out on the children. They need a stable home and your cooperation and support to help them accept their new situation.

Your kids will not stop loving you if they begin appreciating someone else's also taking an interest in their well-being. They'll appreciate you more in the long run for not placing them in a loyalty conflict, or making them feel they must be cold toward their stepmother to prove they are on your side.

For husbands and fathers

Do not entertain the fantasy that your new wife is going to be the "perfect mother" to your child.

Respect the need for distance from each other that is a natural feeling on the part of your children and your new spouse. Remember you are the one who chose a new partner. They did not choose each other.

As the custodial parent, accept the responsibility of being the children's primary caregiver, as you would in the stepmother's absence.

Do not attempt to exclude your ex-wife from her part of the ongoing parenting. This will only backfire on the children, on you, and on your new spouse.

For stepchildren

Your stepmother married your father knowing how important you are to him, and she would like to help him in every aspect of his life, including caring for you.

Your stepmother will be a stranger to you at first, and getting to know her will take time. Try to judge her fairly with your own eyes, and find out if she can be of some help to you.

You have a right to expect your mother to support you in your attempt to become settled within your new family, rather than making you feel uncomfortable or guilty for making an effort.

The new marriage is your father's decision. If you are angry, worried or disturbed about the changes, talk to him about those feelings. Don't take out your discomfort by purposely trying to be as unpleasant as possible to your stepmother. It won't make you feel any better.

The extended family

Do not reject a child because his or her parents are no longer together. Over the long term, people can benefit from any relationship where others show concern.

Parents and step-parents in your family can use your support in providing a warm, caring atmosphere for children who have gone through the upheaval of their parents' separation and divorce.

In some cases of divorce and remarriage, a child may benefit greatly from occasional visits or holidays with sympathetic relatives or friends. A beloved aunt or cousin may be just the person a child feels most comfortable with, so it's important to keep communication open.

Chapter Three

Stepfamily Structures and Legal Issues

The foundation for the stepfamily is laid when the original marriage is dissolved. Since the children remain a part of that biological family forever, divorcing parents who can work out mutually agreeable arrangements for sharing the child care responsibility have taken a major step toward successful adjustment for children and adults at the next stage of their life. When both parents accept ongoing responsibility as single parents for the children's psychological and financial well-being, the pattern can be expected to continue when either or both remarry.

Since the 1968 liberalization of divorce laws in Canada, there has been a considerable increase in the number of divorces. However, most recent Canadian statistics show that 85 per cent of couples have reached an agreement concerning custody and child care arrangements before the divorce enters the legal arena. In fact, these couples are mainly seeking legal confirmation of the completion of one stage of their lives and permission to go on to the next.

Couples who are not able to set aside their emotions, face facts, and work out a pattern of care for their children, have recourse to the adversarial system of the courts. Here again, this method of determining rights and responsibilities will have repercussions on the structure of the remarried family. The court's decision will reflect the family's circumstances at the time of divorce. It cannot be expected to take into account the changes that may occur as children grow and perhaps move informally from one parent to another. The chances of this happening in a fashion that is most healthy for the children appear to be much better in those families where the parents made early attempts to work things out between themselves.

The structure and smooth functioning of a remarried family are inseparable from the legal issues surrounding divorce and children. It is becoming increasingly clear that unresolved issues from the first marriage—and particularly those involving child care—create the most traumatic problems in remarriage. Some of these traumas are not reparable, particularly where children are concerned. If a child has been badly distressed by the absence of a parent, or even more so by the parents' continuing conflicts after the divorce, there is little a step-parent can do to make up for the sense of loss or the loyalty conflicts the children experience at any later date. Preventive measures to protect children's mental health are just as important for a successful remarriage as is the adults' ability to let go of the first relationship in order to pursue a new life. In the legal community and among family counsellors there is a growing awareness that every effort should be made to ensure that a child have continuing contact with both parents and that the parents receive the help they need to protect the children from their anger at one another.

In this chapter, we will consider the impact that the legal system can have on the parents' obligations for their children's psychological well-being; the financial arrangements for their care; and, the wide variety of stepfamily configurations.

Working it Out

The law provides an official stamp of approval to an agreement to end the marriage, but no legal decision can be flexible enough to remain relevant as a family evolves. When a couple first separates, definite rules about visits and obligations help establish some order in ongoing life. As time passes, however, no one should be so tied down by some outside authority that common sense and a loving parent-child relationship are thwarted. There is certainly no need for a rigid rule that a father go on seeing his son every second Tuesday night without fail for ten years, when it would be more appropriate for them to get together for a Saturday afternoon baseball game, a Friday night hockey banquet, or some other events in which they share an interest. Joint custody need not mean trying to split a child's time equally. It should mean taking account of the child's needs along with the adults' needs and capabilities.

As Toronto social worker and divorce mediator Robert McWhinney puts it, mediation is vital for the integrity of the family. Addressing a group of lawyers and social workers in Ottawa in 1983, he stated that there is a growing awareness of the value of mediation between couples because it focuses on the present and future needs of the children, and recognizes that for them the family of origin never ceases to exist. Mediation which encourages the ongoing rapport between parents and children and at least civilized exchanges between former spouses, will allow children to adapt to changing living arrangements while retaining a fond image of their previous families.

Unfortunately, not all couples have the maturity to work out controversial matters at the time of divorce, and some individuals are either emotionally incapable or unwilling to participate in decisions regarding the care of their children. In these cases, as a last resort, the legal system is asked to decide. People caught in the emotional turmoil of failed relationships and readjustment to single life may lose sight of their children's best interests. It is not uncommon or unnatural to seek comfort from a child to combat one's own loneliness, or in the midst of a custody battle with a former spouse. The legal system is therefore called upon in the most difficult situations. When unpopular decisions are made, partners can then blame the courts rather than themselves for failing to come to an agreement. This can relieve tensions temporarily, but it is only just a short-term solution. It is up to the same people who could not arrive at a mutual agreement before resorting to the courts to live up to the agreement now decided for them. But the courts cannot monitor or reinforce essential support for every child.

If the natural mother has never come to terms with her position as the non-custodial parent, she may pursue a psychological battle over the children rather than make the most of her time with them. She can find scapegoats in the legal system, blame her former husband and his new wife for her own unhappiness, and dwell on the custody issue until the children have grown up and it's too late to fight it anymore.

It can sometimes take a long time to have the courts approve changes which have already occurred in a custody situation, but require legal sanction. When Richard, a 33-year-old Cornwall accountant, agreed that two of his four children could live with him because of emotional tensions with their mother, he found he still had to continue paying her child support for all four. Although he was covering living expenses for two at his apartment, she was able to demand payment or their return because she retained legal custody of the children.

Jack, another father who was not awarded custody of his children at the time of divorce, still wished to maintain close ties with them. His new marriage suffered when he could not see his children. When his former wife moved from Montreal to Calgary, taking the children with her, he wanted to reopen the custody issue, particularly since she had become a heavy drinker and he feared for their safety. His lawyers discouraged him from applying.

The previous relationship must be resolved by adults before the children can begin to settle in. It's unreasonable to expect a legal system to work out such a tangled web of feelings, memories and sense of loss. Litigation only increases resentment and does not strengthen the couple's determination to cooperate on the present and future needs of the children.

There have been cases where the legal system has been used by a divorced spouse to periodically revive conflicts. One Ottawa mother, after a bitter divorce, was determined that her two children would have no positive links with their father. He paid alimony and child support for 15 years. Each time the children showed an interest in communicating with him or including him in their lives, she would sue for an increase in the alimony payment, thus creating more turmoil and appealing to the children's loyalty. Eventually the courts recognized the ploy, but not before being taken in for many years and used for purposes that did not help the mental health of the children.

For many years, common lore held that in the event of marital breakdown things would work out as long as one parent took care of the child. We do not agree. There is a growing body of evidence indicating such is not the case. If a stepfamily is to have the opportunity to be stable and happy, an ongoing parent-child relationship with both parents should be worked out in advance. A divorce requiring the assistance of the adversarial system can be a warning signal that does not augur well for the stepfamily.

When the joint parenting has not been left settled, there are repercussions for the children, no matter which parent wins custody. In one family, a mother who had custody of her three children convinced them not to speak to their father. Loyal to their mother, they refused to visit him and his new wife. When the eldest daughter married, he was not invited or informed because the children were convinced he was nothing more than the person who had ruined their mother's life. A mother who does not have custody can also manipulate children's loyalty in a way that makes them feel guilty for preferring to live in a stable household with their dad and stepmother. Instead of feeling comfortable and content with adults who can take care of her needs, a daughter may be so conscious of her mother's "outsider" status that she feels she must take care of her, thus reversing the adult-child relationship. Once again the father is seen as a destroyer of happiness and the poor mother as a victim.

Changes in society's perception of divorce and remarriage are leading to adjustments in the legal system. The process of mediation counselling, where lawyers provide advice on written agreements, means that many more details can be worked out for a family than a judge could ever think

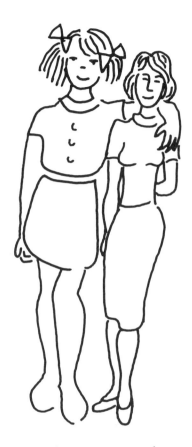

of, let alone decide. As more and more couples follow this avenue for making arrangements concerning their children and property, the legal system will see these cases as examples to emulate.

It is difficult if not impossible to enforce the parent's obligation to care for a child emotionally, but by requiring that both parents contribute to the child's financial support, courts would be indicating to a child that both parents count. It would also signify to each parent that he or she cannot dump his or her responsibilities onto the other, a step-parent or the welfare system. If more and more parents voluntarily take on their responsibilities prior to the final divorce decree, legislators and the courts may make mandatory joint financial and care obligations in the best interests of the child, (as Ontario's family law reform, scheduled to come into effect April 1, 1986, is apparently doing). To date, courts have tended to make decisions based on the children's needs and the parents' rights as they saw them. They have generally absolved the non-custodial father from all but financial responsibility, and the non-custodial mother from any responsibility at all.

When mothers who have legal custody later choose to allow their children to live with their father, the courts are rarely informed. Martha, a Halifax stepmother, and her husband Jim, were happy to have his two daughters spend weekends and summer vacations with them. This arrangement had been in place for two years when Martha married Jim, and it continued smoothly for six years. Then, one weekend, Jan, who was 16, asked if she could move in permanently after the school year ended. She felt close to her father and stepmother and was having difficulty adjusting to her mother's new companion. After discussing the idea, Jim and his former wife agreed to the move, and in July Jan changed households, with goodwill prevailing all round.

So far, governments continue to tolerate default in cases of maintenance orders and require little of non-custodial mothers. Since change usually has to be acceptable to broad segments of society before it is instituted, the effective arrangements that divorcing couples make for themselves will eventually influence the courts' expectations of appropriate behavior in divorcing couples. In the meantime, it can be useful to be aware of the impact of the legal system on the psychological and financial well-being of children in stepfamilies, as well as on the structure of those stepfamilies.

Psychological implications for legal decisions

Legal arrangements do not necessarily reflect the extent and the type of psychological involvement of the natural parents, nor the impact of this involvement on the children. They do indicate some of the expectations. Sometimes the non-custodial parent remains actively involved in the child's life. In other cases, the child rarely comes into contact with the non-custodial parent, or relationships are less than satisfying.

A harmful side effect of the adversarial system for children and adults alike is that in pitting parent against parent, one emerges the winner, the other the loser. If the child is emotionally tied to the parent who is awarded custody, the other parent may be rejected as the wicked figure. This results in a further loss of understanding and a withering relationship. When the child identifies most closely with the parent who does not win custody, the custodial parent may be viewed as a mean, powerful person who wields the disciplinary powers and restricts contact with a powerless victim who, in turn, is so hurt by the loss of the child as to eliminate any future expectations concerning visits, nurturing or financial support.

A child needs ongoing concern from, and contact with, two parents.

Until the 19th century, under English common law, inheritance and property passed from father to children. Thus, in cases of divorce, custody was automatically awarded to the father, who was in a position to ensure their support. With time, the nurturing role associated with motherhood gained importance and the preference for custody shifted to women. Now, with the growing awareness of children's needs to stay in touch with both parents, several types of co-parenting or joint custody arrangements are evolving.

Step-parents have to recognize that non-custodial parents continue to be a part of a child's image and memory of his or her original family. That parent's interaction with the child may or may not have been resolved at the time of divorce. Depending on whether or not the non-custodial parent is accessible, the impact on the children, and therefore on the smooth functioning of the stepfamily, will differ. A biological mother who is physically distant from her children may still maintain links with them through letters, telephone calls, trips and so on. Some natural mothers living in the same town as their children maintain very little contact, if any! Others invest both their time and their emotional energies in providing an alternate home for their children. The natural mother's cooperation or non-cooperation with the children's father and stepmother will influence the stepfamily's ability to respond to the children's needs.

Amy was five when her parents divorced and her mother was granted custody. Now ten, she is often sent to her father's and stepmother's whenever her mother has trouble setting limits on her behavior or getting her to conform. Her father does not feel responsible for setting rules, so she decides her own bedtime and wreaks havoc by leaving dishes everywhere and inviting friends unexpectedly. Her disruptive behavior results in her being sent back to her mother. In effect, while her parents may be cooperating in taking turns with a difficult child, they are not cooperating constructively in giving her the discipline and guidance she needs. Thus, the stepmother felt she had to begin setting limits where the natural parents failed. This was especially difficult since her stepdaughter had been getting away with behavior the stepmother would not have allowed from her own three children, but was still being tolerated by the natural parents. The stepmother was the one who experienced the problem most acutely and finally sought help.

Although a stepmother must accept the legal reality of a co-parenting situation, at times she may also have to bear the brunt of a child's disappointment when parents do not live up to their commitments. It is difficult for courts to ensure that biological parents are meeting their child's needs. They cannot ensure that a child living with his/her father and stepmother regularly visits his/her natural mother, just as they cannot ensure that a child living with the natural mother can easily visit the home of his/her father and stepmother. Yet these opportunities can have significant effects on the smooth functioning and development of emotional ties within the stepfamily. The involvement of other members of the child's extended family following the divorce and remarriage will also help a child's adjustment. As Lilian Messinger of the Clarke Institute in Toronto expresses it, children require "permeable boundaries" which allow them to move freely between either parent's home or among relatives of both parents, where either divorced adult may now feel excluded. In a biological sense, children are part of the extended family as it existed when they were born, and legal decisions should encourage continuing links with both parents.

Some confusing aspects arising within a remarried or blended family do not require a legal solution, simply open and honest discussion and resolution. One of these is the question of different family names within one household. When the Guppy family of father and three children was united with the Thompson family of mother and two children, mother adopted the name Thompson-Guppy while all the children retained their original names. One of children, however, suggested that they all change to either "Ghompson" or "Tuppy", an idea which reflected his feeling that they should present a common front now that they were all part of one family. This would certainly provide one solution to the question of some bills being addressed to Mr. Guppy and others to Mrs. Thompson, or hockey notices for the stepmother's son addressed to the stepfather with the assumption that they share the same last name.

For some families, legal adoption may appear to be an attractive option to help children feel they are a part of the remarried family. While this communicates a step-parent's (usually a stepfather's) commitment to a child, it does not magically transform the household into a nuclear family. If such is the intent, in hindsight it probably will be viewed as a failure.

Although historically 25 per cent of adoptions have been to step-parents, the present trend is to fewer adoptions of this kind. Names can be legally changed without recourse to adoption. Also, it is very important not to underestimate a child's attachment to his birth name and the ties to the parent that go with it.

Another consideration is that adoption is more available to men who would be giving their name to a stepchild, than to women who probably would not. At the present time, an adult moving into a household with children not his or her own has no legal rights over them. On the other hand, he or she may be recognized as legally liable for those children. A form of guardianship with clearly defined rights and responsibilities would help families understand step-parenting obligations. Such a written statement of the step-parent's guardian status would constitute tangible evidence of the acceptance of certain bonds. Above all, the guardian would be viewed as an *additional* adult caring for the children, not a replacement for a parent or a means of excluding a parent.

Children are very anxious to discover who they are and what fashioned them, especially during the teen years, so cutting off their ties with the past can have serious repercussions. One Kingston doctor who became a stepfather of a 10-year-old boy when he married, adopted him when it became clear the natural father wanted no continuing ties. The adoption was undertaken with the kindest of intentions, and the history of the situation was not kept from the boy. By the time he was 15, however, it became apparent that the issue was not resolved as far as he was concerned; he attempted to contact his natural father and was rejected several times. When he finally did succeed in meeting him, he was granted only five minutes. This experience proved so painful that he vented his anger and sadness by defying his stepfather. The situation was slowly resolved with time and counselling, but it might have been avoided had the mother and stepfather earlier recognized the boy's need to acknowledge that he did in fact have a natural father, whose history he shared. Moving into a new household can be enough of an adjustment for a child without losing his name as well.

Financial Implications of Legal Decisions

Although it is difficult if not impossible for the courts to enforce measures that will ensure the psychological well-being of a child following divorce of the parents, economic well-being is more easily monitored. However, even if both partners have accepted some financial responsibility for their child, the courts are not likely to pursue a defaulting parent unless the child is seen to be deprived as a consequence of the parent's failure to provide financial assistance. In practice, this means that the courts often assume that the children of a woman who remarries will be supported by her new husband, and the natural father will generally not be pursued to make support payments. Similarly, the non-custodial mother is rarely ordered by the courts to help support her children, even if her financial circumstances would allow her to do so. In these cases, the stepfather or the stepmother is subsidizing their partner's children, which can mean quite a hefty burden. Usually the law does not concern itself with the family's budget unless the child is in need.

In a remarried family, the implications of how money is spent are important. Sometimes it is not possible or advisable to maintain separate financial arrangements for each spouse, particularly when children are still living at home and both spouses share in household expenses. Nonetheless, biological and emotional ties make a difference in who buys special gifts for the children. The traditional financial arrangement between spouses involving complete sharing of incomes will not work when a natural father wants to spend a large sum for a vacation with his children whom he sees only infrequently, and the stepmother sees the need to stretch the budget to cover the cost of a new furnace. Since the priorities of a remarried couple will not always match, recognizing the right to maintain separate financial accounts can help minimize conflict over spending. Emotional attachment and a sense of commitment to one's own children will indicate priorities, so it is not inappropriate to keep money aside for such expenses. Other books tackle the budget issues for remarried couples more extensively, and can give more guidance on sharing the financial obligations fairly.

Do step-parents have a financial obligation toward the children of their spouse? It appears society still expects that a man marrying a woman with children will "rescue" the one-parent family both emotionally and financially, and relieve the non-custodial father of his emotional and financial responsibility for his children. The law, unfortunately, colludes in this arrangement with the best interests of the children in mind. It looks at the joint budget of the remarried couple rather than assuming that the non-custodial parent continues to have obligations. The fact that the couple might want to allocate its budget on other things besides children's food, clothing and orthodontic fees is not considered. Nor is the fact that even by paying only a small amount each month, the non-custodial parent would be demonstrating his or her commitment to the child.

Non-custodial mothers have rarely been required to pay any child support, but this sex-biased attitude of the courts appears to be slowly changing. Eighty-five per cent of the mothers retain custody, and those who do not are often unable to contribute financially to their children. In one Windsor family, Lynn, 35, who had found a highly paid position since her divorce, agreed out of court to pay substantial monthly support for her three children. They had been in their father's custody for five years and she had contributed very little at first. When her former husband asked her to start doing so on a regular basis, she thought that was unreasonable. However, after considering the excellent parenting he had provided, she realized his request was fair, since he would continue to have full time responsibility for the children's care.

As more women enter the labour force, a periodic case-by-case reassessment by an objective body would allow flexibility in the financial arrangements. At the moment there is no automatic process for review. The decision made at the time of the divorce stands, unless the children are deprived or the custodial parent chooses to reopen the legal battle. Considering the emotional turmoil that may be involved for the children if their parents go through another skirmish over money, avoiding reassessment may be in the best interests of the child. However, a stepmother who helps to pay for items such as underwear and cod liver oil is at a distinct disadvantage compared to a non-custodial mother who provides special gifts such as watches, suits and even a car. One father complained that when his children visited their mother, he had to send the groceries along with them. And he did! This leads to bad feelings on the part of the father, guilt for the children and anger for the stepmother. If, at the time of divorce, parents were expected to accept joint financial responsibility for the children, even if their respective contributions differed, children would see them both as supporters.

A step-parent's financial obligations to stepchildren are not clearly defined. If a parent dies, the step-parent is usually expected to continue with the care of the child as he or she has been doing. In the case of second marriages which end in divorce—and 47 percent do—the step-parent can often be held liable for ongoing financial support, even if the natural parent, especially the father, never provided child support on a regular basis. Step-parents usually contribute a great deal to the financial'well-being of the children, particularly when they are still living at home. The courts can therefore take the position that they have accepted an implied financial obligation, even in the absence of a legal judgement. As some step-parents have found, the more they do, the less the natural parent is obliged to do.

The impact of legal decisions on the structure of the stepfamily

The situation at the termination of a marriage will, as we have seen, have repercussions on the structure of the remarried family. However, because families grow and change, legal decisions made at the time of divorce do not always accurately reflect the situation as time passes. Many custody changes are arranged informally without going back to the courts for legal confirmation. This makes it difficult to obtain accurate data on the true custodial practices of divorced parents, and it is unreasonable to rely totally on custody award statistics to determine how many children live with either parent. The official records do not tell the whole story, or reveal the hidden numbers of stepmothers who are caring for their husband's children even though they are still legally in the custody of their natural mother.

It is a measure of the invisibility of the stepfamily, and the stepmother in particular, that data pertaining directly to them is not gathered. The figures we present below are based on two recent studies of divorce in Canada. Our calculations are of necessity indirect, and the figures are not necessarily fully compatible or consistent. Also, because the family situation in Canada varies from year to year and from region to region, the numbers provide only a rough approximation.

The number of divorces granted annually in Canada increased rapidly after the liberalization of the divorce law in 1968, from 50 per 100,000 population to about 250 per 100,000 population by 1979. This represents some 60,000 divorces in 1979, given Canada's population of 24 million at the time. Of these divorces, about half involved dependent children. Where custody was in question, men obtained custody in about one seventh of the cases. So, in 1979, one-fourteenth of the divorces—4,500 overall in the country—resulted in the creation of a single-parent household headed by a male.

It is believed that about 80 per cent of divorced men remarry, and that the vast majority of these marriages occur about 18 months after divorce. For the purposes of our calculation, we will assume that the same proportion of divorced men with children remarry as those without, and that they do so at a fixed period of about two years after divorcing. By also assuming that the rate of creation of single-parent families with male heads, the percentage of these male heads who remarry, and the time distribution of their remarriages all remain constant for the period, we can calculate the number of women who become stepmothers each year by marrying divorced men with custody of dependent children. On the basis of the 1979 data, it is simply 4,500 x 0.8, or 3,600 new stepmothers across Canada. To calculate the number of children involved, Statistics Canada figures show that the total number of children involved in divorce cases is about the same as the number of divorces themselves. Because only half the divorces involve dependent children, on average there will be two children associated with each divorce of a parent of dependent children, and subsequently with the number of male-headed single households that become stepfamilies. Therefore, approximately 7,200 dependent children in Canada acquire stepmothers each year. If we approximate the total number of women who have become stepmothers since the liberalization of the divorce laws, we find that the 505,000 divorces from 1969 to 1979 would result in 30,200 stepmothers. With an average two children per remarriage, about 60,000 children in Canada acquired stepmothers in this period. Since the divorce rate increased rapidly in the decade following 1969 and appears to have stabilized at a higher level in the early 1980s, the number of new stepmothers over the decade 1979 to 1989 will no doubt be higher than the previous decade.

These calculations, limited as they are, give an approximate idea of the number of women in Canada who are actively caring for dependent stepchildren. The figures are restricted to women who become stepmothers by marrying men who have custody of all their children following a divorce. Since the data is not available, they do not take into account the number of women who marry widowers with children; women who take over the stepmother role even though their husbands do not have legal custody; and, those arrangements where there is legal or *de facto* joint custody over one or more children, or where the custody of two or more children is split between the parents. Women who have a stable partnership with men with children, but are not legally married, are also excluded from the statistics.

Types of stepfamily structures

There are many types of stepfamily and blended family arrangements, and different time configurations for these arrangements, such as weekdays, weekends, summer holidays and so on. Our intent here is not to describe them all in detail, simply to give some highlights and examples that illustrate the complexity.

A person can be part of a stepfamily without consciously acknowledging it. Several stepmothers included in a Queensway-Carleton Hospital study in Ottawa indignantly denied they were stepmothers to their husband's children. They claimed to be mothers, since they saw themselves as occupying a full fledged maternal role.

Attempting to disguise such a household as a nuclear family means that its members deny differences that are evident from the time they get up in the morning until they go to bed at night. They choose to nourish three marvelous myths about stepfamilies: 1. Recreating a nuclear family will re-establish the safe, loving family that went wrong the first time; 2. By excluding the non-custodial parent, the children will forget him or her and replace that person with a new dad or mom; and 3. The harder they work at establishing closeness and intimacy, the better things will be.

No matter how much the stepfamily may masquerade as a nuclear family or attempt to mask its origins, and no matter how much members of a stepfamily would like it to be a nuclear family, a close look at the structure of the stepfamily will reveal how impossible it is to *be* a nuclear family. They *look* different, they *function* differently, they *are* different.

The various types of stepfamilies, from the stepmother's perspective, are determined by five key variables:

1. The presence and number of children of either partner:
   a) his and hers
   b) his and not hers
   c) his and hers and joint
   d) his and joint

2. Residential arrangements:
   a) his children
      • all live with him
      • some live with him
      • none live with him
   b) her children
      • all live with her
      • some live with her
      • none live with her
      • has none

3. Visiting arrangements:
   a) his children (residential)

       (non-residential)

   b) her children (residential)

       (non residential)

- visit mother
- do not visit
- visit father
- do not visit
- visit father
- do not visit
- visit mother
- do not visit

4. Age of stepchildren:
   a) under twelve years
   b) adolescent
   c) young adult
   d) adult

5. Marital status at the time of remarriage:
   a) husband
   b) wife

- widowed
- divorced
- widowed
- divorced
- single

The first variable that affects the structure of the stepfamily is a biological one: who are the children, to whom do they belong? There are four possibilities, all of which include the man's children if there is a stepmother in the picture: the family with his children, while she has none; the family with his children and her children; the family with his children, her children and their joint children; and, the family with his children and their joint children.

The next variable is residential arrangements. Here the children of the husband and wife have to be considered separately. Do all his children live with him, only some, or none of them? Do all her children live with her, some only, or none?

The third variable determining family structure is more complicated—the visiting or "change of residence" arrangements. Here we have to consider the children who live in the home of the stepfamily and visit the other parent's home, as well as those who live elsewhere and come to visit or refuse to visit. If the children are independent, they may still consider their father's house "home," while the stepmother may consider their stay a visit.

The fourth element is the age of the children. There will be different style families depending on whether the children are under 12 and need a lot of care or if they are adolescents, young adults or grown up sons and daughters at the time of the remarriage. The stepfamily arrangement may vary periodically, depending upon changes in custody or visiting patterns, unlike nuclear families where most change is due to natural growth and aging. Changes in visiting patterns or residences can affect the stepfamily differently from week to week or year to year, and different ages and developmental stages must be considered in making some of these arrangements.

The fifth variable that can introduce more or less complexities in the stepfamily is the marital status or each partner prior to the remarriage. The man may have been widowed or divorced, the stepmother single, widowed or divorced.

This simplified listing may appear complicated to the uninitiated, but the point is a stepfamily is not as simple as a nuclear family. There are many possible variations. For example, did the children's other parent remarry? Is the visiting arrangement regular or not? Is the non-custodial parent in town or even in the country? All of these factors can affect the outcome of the remarried family, as can a new child born to the non-custodial parent, or a remarriage which occurs after a third or fourth divorce. There is such a wide range of possibilities that if a stepmother is planning to run the show or to assume the responsibility of providing for the children's emotional well-being of all, she must face the fact that her life cannot possibly be the same as that of a mother in a nuclear family.

Emily B. Visher, Ph.D. and John Visher M.D. of Palo Alto, California, have spent years studying and conducting workshops for stepfamilies. They have outlined several characteristics of these families:

1. All the individuals have suffered many important losses: relationships, community, dreams and fantasies of marital life.
2. All individuals in a stepfamily have previous family histories.
3. Parent-child relationships predate the new couple relationship.
4. There is a biological parent elsewhere in actuality or in memory with power and influence over family members.
5. Children are members of two households if they have contact with both parents.
6. Little, if any, legal relationship exists between step-parents and stepchildren.

Regardless of the residential arrangements at any given time, these characteristics serve to ensure that the stepfamily continues to be a different entity from a biological one. Of course, depending on which children live with which parent, and the degree of interaction, methods of working out daily routines will vary greatly from one stepfamily to another. Coping with more people is one of the initial tasks.

The Vishers have shown in graphic style the sheer numbers involved when parents divorce and remarry. Consider: Mary and John have a nuclear family. There are eight people in this family, including two sets of grandparents and Mary and John's two children. The number of possible interactions among eight people is 247. If Mary and John divorce and Mary remarries Bill, who has three children from his first marriage, the number of interactions increases tremendously. At this point, we have one stepfamily and one single-parent household, with a total of 17 people. Later John remarries Joan, a widow with one child. There are now two stepfamilies consisting of 23 people connected by shared children. The potential number of interactions is 8,388,584. This figure demonstrates the complexity and confusion that can exist in stepfamilies simply as a function of the number of people involved. Each of these people may feel that he or she has some reason to influence the course of the stepfamily. This complexity often works against the stepfamily's ability to form a stable, cohesive unit with clear boundaries.

Stepfamilies find that they must function differently just to keep up with the complications of changing residences, ages and needs of children at different times, and the fact that the family expands and contracts differently than a nuclear family. As we have stated earlier, this complexity and the flexibility it requires of stepfamilies has to be seen as the starting point for working out such matters as the care of the children, their discipline, and the role of the extended family.

Despite the great variety of structure and make-up of stepfamilies, they share many common characteristics, and children are strikingly aware of them. For many children who have two places to call home, there is in fact no one place that feels like home now that the intimacy of the single-parent household has been altered by the addition of the parent's new partner.

For Jenny, a 14-year-old Toronto student, "flexibility" means that she lives with her dad until he gets tired of her; then she moves to her mom's until she cannot stand being there any longer; next she goes to her grandmother's for a while, before starting the circuit back to her father. This so-called flexibility, which requires that a child wander among family members, demonstrates a lack of commitment to the child. Although the parameters and value of equally shared custody remains to be measured, parental commitment determines a child's well-being and future far more than the details of living arrangements.

Seventeen-year-old Marie, who lives near Ottawa, laughs when asked to count all her relatives. She chose to live with her father when she began feeling tremendous pressure from her mother to accept her new stepfather as her own father, and to try to behave as though her stepfamily were her original family. Her father's new wife, her stepmother, does not try to take her natural mother's place, and that feels more comfortable to Marie. Her stepmother's sons come to visit her father's home on weekends, and her father and stepmother have a small child, a half-sister of whom Marie is very fond. When she goes to see her mother, her visits often coincide with those of her stepfather's sons, who live with their mother but feel at home in both households. In either of Marie's parents' homes, the persons present in a family portrait would simply reflect the day of the week or time of the year!

The "absent" parent

The stepfamily's make-up includes the non-custodial parent, whether or not on-going contact exists between her and her children. An absent father is more often acknowledged in the literature of stepfamilies than an absent mother. He is seen to be statistically more common, and perhaps this is the reason more interest has been focused on him.

Very little has been written about the absent or neglectful mother, and the effect on the children. Children can find it too painful to solve the mystery of her absence without admitting that she is consciously and purposefully rejecting them. Perhaps they want to believe that the father is standing in the way of visits and letters. Maybe the stepmother is suspected as part of the plot, a plan to keep the mother away. Without the presence of the natural mother, the stepmother's position is tenuous at best. The children, whose self-esteem is undermined by their mother's absence, often target their anxiety by being hostile toward the stepmother.

Some parents who would prefer to drop their obligations toward their children are not honest about their feelings. Anne, at 12, stayed with her father after his divorce. She had always sought his attention, and throughout her adolescence was quite happy to have her mother out of the way so she could share a home with her Dad. But her little partner role ended when her father decided to remarry. He did not know how to deal with his loyalty conflicts between Anne and his new wife, so he attempted to retain his loving father image while at the same time trying to strengthen his new marriage by getting Anne to move out of the house. He accomplished this by moving to Europe temporarily, knowing that Anne would reasonably choose to stay behind in Toronto to finish high school, and that this would require her moving in with her mother. The problem was that Anne totally refused to recognize her father's rejection. She literally made herself ill worrying that she was the one who had rejected her father by choosing to remain in Canada. She lost weight, became very depressed and finally sought psychiatric help.

Mary, an Edmonton secretary, is another absent parent who transferred her responsibility onto her child. Mary decided her nerves were so destroyed by losing the custody battle and living without her son that the only solution was to move to California where she could forget him. Her nine-year-old, Tim, felt he could not tell her how much he would miss her since she had already explained she was at the breaking point. He was made to feel that if he wished her to stay nearby, he was wishing her to suffer for him. Without his mother, and with his self-imposed restraint on saying he needed her, Tim grew up not knowing how to develop close ties with anyone. By the time he was in his twenties, it was becoming clear to him that he had really missed a large part of the nurturing he needed. His stepmother had been the only mother figure in his life, but his mother, who never came back, took Tim's trust with her. Rather than confiding his sadness and loneliness to anyone, he stood like a little soldier protecting his memory of a loving mother who left him only because she cared about him too much.

Illness can also result in the absence of a parent. When a custodial father suffers a serious illness, which requires a lengthy stay in hospital, it can create a serious gap between stepmother and stepchildren in the home. His presence has been counted on and his guidance expected. At such a time, the non-custodial parent can play a very important part, providing the emotional backup to children or teens that their stepmother cannot effectively give. Members of the extended family can also provide the required support in such circumstances. Unfortunately this is still the exception.

Occasionally children are taught to reject their non-custodial parent. Charles, a 40-year-old electrician in Winnipeg, left his wife and two children after years of friction. She succeeded in turning their two children completely against him, so that they blamed him for breaking up the family. When he remarried, the children refused to see him anymore. He waited 10 years, never forgetting a birthday or Christmas gift, and finally one of his sons, now 20, met him for lunch; the second son appears almost ready to follow suit.

Grown-up stepchildren in the family structure

When children are grown up at the time of remarriage, there is no custody battle, no problems checking out visiting arrangements with the other parent, and no money to be paid for child support. However, ghosts of the past are still very much present, and the special relationship between father and adult children can exclude the stepmother to a greater extent than in the case of youngsters. Since the growing years are completed, she will have no contribution to make to them, and consequently no memories to share with her husband of milestones and poignant incidents.

Of course, she will likely also be spared the projected anger of children who miss their mother, and any blame for disrupting their home. Although they may still feel a desire to visit, the home is not theirs as adults in the same way it is to younger people.

Even so, it can be quite disconcerting to visit, even as a mature woman, and find your father's home altered. This happened to Suzanne, 42, married with her own three children. She visited her father one Easter with many of the same expectations she had when her mother was still living there. But the house was not the same after Alice moved in to share father's life. Although Suzanne's mother had moved out years earlier, she had left her stamp, and Suzanne had helped to perpetuate many of the family traditions and gatherings. But now the kitchen smells were different, the pictures on the walls had been changed, and the furniture rearranged to suit the remarried couple's tastes. Alice's adult children also joined them for these family occasions. Even though they were very pleasant, Suzanne could not help feeling they did not belong in her parents' house. She was happy for her father, but Alice's chances of becoming a member of Suzanne's family were very slim. Alice was the outsider, the intruder, and felt it keenly when her husband's family came to visit. In some ways, no matter how much she wanted the marriage, she was sorry she gave up her old home where she could celebrate Easter and other holidays with her own children and grandchildren.Suzanne's family, though they felt resentful, were at least polite enough to attempt to include Alice and to show their appreciation for her baking and other preparations. Other step-children are not so supportive.

At 38, Christina is another adult who had not come to terms with her parents' divorce which took place when she was 14. Her mother did not adjust well following the end of her marriage. Her father, however, found happiness with his new wife Ellen, and had been married 10 years. That did not prevent Christina from thinking that her father made a mistake divorcing her mother, and trying several ways of getting them back together. The latest attempt was at the confirmation of her 13-year-old son, Joey. She suggested that a formal picture of the parents and grandparents with Joey would be appropriate, clearly excluding her stepmother. Ellen made up her mind that she would attend no more family occasions until Christina came to terms with the reality of her father's second marriage.

The ideal situation for all concerned, children and adults, is when the stepmother enters an already established amicable working arrangement between the natural parents for the children care.

When Kay, at 30, recognized that her marriage had resulted in her losing touch with her own strengths and in resentment at her husband's possessiveness, she felt the only solution was to move out and get on her own feet. She recognized that her husband, David, was a devoted father and a good role model for their five-year-old son, Jamie. So she left them both and took a room just a few blocks away from their Burnaby home while she looked for a job. The couple came to a cooperative parenting agreement which allowed them both the freedom to pursue an individual social life and to take care of Jamie according to his needs and their own. Kay took him to swimming lessons, welcomed him when he visited and brought his friends, and kept him overnight if David was going to be out late. For Jamie, this access to both parents was comforting, and the fact that they had no other interaction with each other was not a problem for him. However volatile each partner's feelings were at any particular time, they were each able to continue the cooperative parenting.

Two years after the separation, when David was seriously considering remarrying, Kay's initial reaction was one of overwhelming jealousy and strong feelings against another woman developing a closeness with her child. Following much soul-searching and counselling, she began to realize that her special relationship with Jamie would not be threatened by a new person in David's life. Also, her own new companion would be no threat to Jamie's bond with his father. The more freedom each adult has to pursue his or her life, the better the emotional climate for their child.

A stepmother entering David and Jamie's life will find a child who does not have to cope with conflicts between his parents. The movement back and forth between two households takes some getting used to, as do the daily phone calls to or from his mother. On the other hand, Kay is still buying Jamie's clothes, and since his new stepmother is not overwhelmed with parenting responsibilities, she has the time to learn how to relate to her stepchild.

In most chapters we include do's and don'ts in our recommendations. Here we prefer to stress the importance of not looking for a winner and a loser in the custody question. We prefer to speak of working together to resolve issues, to the point where both partners are comfortable with the arrangement and the new family can move ahead productively.

Recommendations

For the step-parent—issues to consider:
1. Remember, you are not a "second class citizen."
2. The reality of legal and biological ties must be respected.
3. Your participation and contribution will define your role more than any legal mandate.
4. Being a stepmother means making a contribution to the lives of your husband's children.

Natural father—issues to consider:
1. Unresolved attachments to your ex-spouse can interfere with the happiness of your new marriage. This is sometimes disguised by a thin facade of legal obligations.
2. Your legal responsibilities should be taken seriously; they will instill a sense of stability in your children.
3. Fluidity and flexibility of family members participating in significant events cannot be defined by law. Take each occasion as it comes and work it out in a responsible way. This will sometimes include your new spouse, sometimes the ex-spouse, occasionally both.
4. As the children grow, there will be a need for some adjustments to access and living arrangements. The needs of both parents and child should be considered in finding the best solutions.

Non-custodial natural mother—issues to consider:
1. Continued participation and responsibility for your child are important.
2. Cooperation with the custodial parent will help your child.
3. Accept that the original nuclear family is changed, although it still exerts a strong influence on its former members, especially the children. They now have an expanded network and you have a responsibility to help them in their adjustment.

Chapter Four

The Extended Family

One summer weekend, Joanne, an Ottawa nurse, was expecting 25 of her relatives for dinner. At the same time, her son was leaving to visit his father and to join in the annual reunion of that side of his family. Although her husband, Max, was staying in town to help host the dinner, his own children had the option of going to their cottage. This would give them an opportunity to spend some time with their mother who had also remarried and was vacationing at a nearby cottage .

On a neighboring street, Eva was welcoming her aunt and uncle from Czechoslovakia. This was the beginning of a month in which the busy research chemist would be hostess as well as interpreter. Even though they could not speak each other's language, the visitors received a warm welcome from Eva's Canadian husband and his children from a former marriage. The husband's family joined in to make sure the visiting couple had an opportunity to see many of the points of interest around the national capital.

Not every gathering proceeds so smoothly for members of remarried families. Jim, a respected surgeon in Toronto, was 35 when he married Jill three years after his divorce. As an X-ray technician and part of the medical team at the same Toronto hospital, she had worked with Jim for several years. She had had many opportunities to get to know his two children while he had been caring for them on his own. The couple was happy with their new status, and Jim was sure his parents shared his feelings. However, during summer weekends at his parents' cottage, it was obvious this was not the case. His mother would ask Jill to bring food, then would not serve it. She frequently mentioned her continuing sadness about her son's divorce and refused to accept Jill as her son's new partner and as a new parental figure for her grandchildren.

Divorce is a breakdown of a nuclear family, but it is a great deal more. All of a couple's friends and relatives are affected to some degree. They will have to work through their feelings concerning this change before they can see where they belong in the new situation. In the meantime, children of every age need continuity; and for this they look to the adults in their lives. When two parents decide to live apart, they nevertheless continue to be parents together.

Grandparents are still grandparents; aunts and uncles continue to have the same blood relationship with their nieces and nephews. A sense of family identity and belonging should not be altered by a legal statement awarding one parent custody of the children. The other parent remains a parent, and members of both parents' families are still important to the children.

In this chapter, we will consider the impact of the extended family on the children of the stepfamily, on the remarried couple, and on the family dynamics. Building up new relationships takes time, especially for children. Maintaining ties with both natural families is very important because other people cannot take the place of a parent, a grandparent or a cousin.

Who belongs to the extended stepfamily? Everyone has different ties and different perspectives. From the children's point of view, their first family includes two parents and four grandparents. With divorce and remarriage, the new people who enter their lives are members of their extended family. From the stepmother's point of view, her husband's family, including his ex-wife who remains the stepchildren's parent, are the extended family members. Here we include all these people as members of the extended family, although from the point of view of some, they are also original family members.

In any case, the extended family means people—lots of people. Far from being orphans, sometimes the children in a stepfamily have more relatives than they can sort out. There are their biological parents and one or two step-parents. In addition to their four biological grandparents, there can also be another four persons who may or may not wish to be considered grandparents. Then, along with their own siblings, they might have two sets of stepbrothers and stepsisters—those they live with and those they visit. Add to all of these people their original aunts, uncles and cousins, and those they have acquired through a parent's remarriage. Then there are the new and old families, close friends who may be in contact more often than relatives, earning them status as members of the extended family also. Friends can sometimes serve as buffers as well, simply because they are not relatives.

Following the divorce and the grief it can cause many family members, there is often an unsettled period when relatives and friends are hesitant to take sides. During this period it is difficult to keep the children's particular needs in mind. Because the children will in all likelihood be living with one parent, that parent's relatives and friends may become overly involved at first.At the same time, relatives of the non-custodial parent may withdraw, fearing a rebuff or feeling they are no longer wanted or needed. If these family ties are to continue into a remarriage, they must not be allowed to wither during the single-parent phase.

Then, when a new family is formed with one or two sets of children, there follows the long process of getting to know not only the stepmother but also those relatives and friends important to her. The stepmother must also meet those people who are close to the stepchildren. There are no common, accepted terms to describe these new relationships, no familial word for the young woman who is your stepmother's sister, and no rules about what to call the man who is your stepfather's father. These people do not replace the original family's aunt or grandfather, but they may turn out to be good friends. By maintaining an appropriate distance initially, and by not assuming immediate acceptance, the step-parent's relatives and friends can allow children the time they need to get to know them at their own pace.

Separation doesn't end parenting

When a marriage ends, the biological and psychological bonds between the parent and child live on. Every adult has some responsibility for the child to whom he or she is related. The custodial parent's first support in the parenting role should naturally be the child's other parent. Unfortunately a uniform code of ethics regarding the obligations of the non-custodial parent has not yet been developed. Court decisions that spell out parental rights are not capable of enforcing appropriate behavior, and the adversary system that gives one parent legal custody still appears to be labelling one parent good, the other bad. As we explained in the chapter on the legal system and stepfamilies, children can easily become pawns in divorce proceedings. The increasing numbers of parents seeking joint custody at the time of divorce is an encouraging sign reflecting a growing awareness of the ongoing responsibility of parenting after marital breakdown.

It takes a conscious effort to put the interests of the children first when one parent may be feeling rejected, blamed and unwanted, and the other, feeling stronger, is reluctant to depend on the ex-spouse to carry out promises to their children. There are some parents who do not have custody of their children simply because they do not want to. They have chosen to absent themselves physically and even emotionally; preoccupied with their own needs, they are available to their children only when it does not interfere with their own plans. But children need to keep in touch with the non-custodial natural parent as part of their own healthy development. Parents who recognize this fact will also help the child maintain contact with the extended family.

Grandparents, like the children of divorcing parents, usually prefer to keep the family intact. They need time to grieve the loss of their child's marriage before they can support any new relationship in his or her life. Grandparents who are close to their grandchildren and have a balanced view of the marital breakdown can be a crucial link to their heritage for the children.

Usually grandparents will stand by their own child even if they are saddened by the break-up of the marriage, but this isn't always the case. In one Canadian family recently, the husband's parents were so angered by their son's separation from his wife that they disowned him. Now his wife and the two daughters in her custody are welcome in their home, but the husband and 12-year-old son in his custody are *persona non grata*. In effect, a young boy has now been cut off from his grandparents.

Given time to overcome their sense of loss, grandparents who keep in touch with their grandchildren can provide needed support and assistance. However, it is not necessary for them to be quite as effusive as the grandmother who told her teenage grand-daughters she was very proud of them for being able to live with a stepmother!

A question of loyalties

As family members and friends try to work out their loyalties to the divorced couple, they may either become overly involved or withdraw from the children. In some instances, the extended family steps in after the break. The family of the non-custodial parent can make sure the children stay in touch with their part of the family, as well as provide support to the single parent. However, such intense involvement can be shortlived, forcing the children to adjust once more to the loss of opportunities to be with people they love.

If parents of the divorced couple find it trying to keep up cordial relations with their former daughter-in-law or son-in-law, remarriage on either side can make it even more difficult. Sometimes the bitterness is so profound that contact with grandchildren is absolutely minimal.

Julia, a Kitchener, Ontario stepmother, occasionally hears her three stepdaughters speak of their mother's parents in Austria. During the six years Julia has been with them, the grandparents have not communicated with the girls. Their father has made no attempt to reassure his former in-laws that he would appreciate their continuing contact with the children. This he left with their mother, who may or may not have encouraged her parents to write. No matter whether it's shyness on the part of the grandparents, inattention from the natural parents, or other reasons, both children and grandparents are being denied an opportunity for rewarding personal contact and growth.

There are times when a relative does make a point of seeing the children often and serving as a link between the children's life in the stepfamily and their visits to the other parent.

Michael, an engineer in Burnaby, B.C., has custody of his children. He keeps in regular touch with his Aunt Mary, who is also a good friend of his former wife, Elsa. So when the children visit their mother, aunt Elsa is often there as well, acting as a buffer and helping to keep things less emotional and easier for everyone. Because she maintains contact with both sides of the family, she makes it possible for the children to talk about school and daily patterns of activities without feeling disloyal to the adults.

At times friends also face a dilemma in knowing how to respond to the blended family. There is no established etiquette, and friends and neighbors can feel that showing any interest or friendliness toward the new stepfamily indicates disrespect to the former spouse. Sometimes getting to know the new partner helps all concerned feel more comfortable, but there are no guarantees. Friendly ties cannot continue if people refuse to recognize the fact that things have changed, whether they like it or not.

The extended stepfamily

The day-to-day activities and feelings in the stepfamily are not necessarily determined by bloodlines, but rather by the adult relationships involved. A new step-parent brings not only relatives but also close friends to the new family. In some cases, a child may find it easier to build a strong relationship with one of these people than with the step-parent. On the other hand, any hostility a child has toward a step-parent may also be directed at other members of that step-parent's family. A child or teenager who deeply feels the loss of an absent parent cannot find a substitute for that parent in the extended family. He may build other friendships, but he may also cope with his hurt and sadness by striking out at the step-parent, or by extension at a member of her family. Grandparents can be a prime target. Anxious to be part of the children's world, they may hurt the children's feelings when least expected. One step-grandmother, who came to live with her daughter's family in Montreal, did not realize that her enthusiasm for taking photos of her new step-grandchildren to send to her friends could be seen an imposition. The children put up with her, but made no attempt to hide their resentment, and she learned quickly that they felt she was an intruder. Rather than try to force the issue or demand pseudo-affection, this stepmother's mother retreated a little. She now maintains a polite distance, with which everyone is comfortable.

Trying to bridge this distance when a stepchild is not ready is a mistake, even though the attempt may appear logical to adults. A child who is feeling abandoned by his own parent may not be able to express this in

words, but he may need to withdraw for a time from other members of the stepfamily.

The fact of the matter is that a stepmother cannot provide for the complete range of the child's emotional needs, no matter how hard she tries.

Some children choose their own adult to be close to. Carol, a stepmother in Granby, Quebec, is fortunate that her sister Donna is a special favorite of her stepdaughter. Seven-year-old Christine enjoys visiting her new aunt at her farm on weekends. The positive feelings she may have for her stepmother can be demonstrated much more openly to Donna since this does not make the child feel disloyal to her own natural mother. For Emily, a 15-year-old, it is much easier to show affection toward her stepmother's friend Claire, than toward her stepmother. The teenager loves to babysit at Claire's house, where she feels at home, perhaps because she finds the distance she is seeking.

Children need their families

Divorce and remarriage change the makeup of the family for each child.

It may be tempting to appeal to concepts such as fairness and to talk about which parent deserves to have more influence over a child, but the biological connection is a part of him or her and it is wrong to force a child to reject it. In some stepfamilies, it may be uncomfortable to mention some of the children's physical characteristics or mannerisms that remind the custodial parent of the ex-spouse. Contact with the ex-spouse's side of the family allows the child to talk about some of these inherited characteristics, like the shape of a chin, the naturally curly hair, or the ability to tell rib-cracking jokes with a straight face. It is important to allow children to keep in touch with those friends and relatives who make them feel worthwhile and comfortable. On the other hand, there is no need to push relatives on them if there is no mutual interest in keeping in touch or if they just do not happen to get along. But neither are there logical grounds for cutting them off from a chance to find out. Blocking off one part of a child's family will not help him or her adapt to new living arrangements.

Of course, with this agreement to keep in touch with all members of their family, the children will be crossing family boundaries that adults can no longer cross because of the change in their marital status. It takes trust and a strong commitment to the children's welfare on the part of all the adults who care about them, especially the custodial parent and the step-parent. But it can work to everyone's advantage when a child feels he/she belongs to a large family that loves him.

One Calgary stepmother reported: "The kids may go down to Texas this Christmas with their mother, and that's what I really hope will happen. They will come back knowing that they didn't just fall from a tree, that they have roots and connections somewhere. Although they don't get much direct care from their mother, there are all these family members they share with her. They will have an affinity toward each other and get more of a sense of their identity."

It is a wonderful feeling for a child to know somebody thinks he or she is special. When a child can keep in touch with real members of the extended family, he or she will not have to look for imaginary ones.

One should keep in mind, however, that just because all these relatives exist does not necessarily mean any or all will stay in touch with the children without a little prodding. Sometimes a blended family can look so complete on its own, with two parents and two sets of children, that relatives need to be asked before they realize their support would be appreciated. A parent and a step-parent can provide a home, but they cannot operate in isolation and provide all the emotional warmth each child must have.

The stepfamily really should not have to be left on its own, considering the large number of other persons who are potential allies in caring for the children. Simple arithmetic shows that, (as Visher and Visher presented in 1980 to the Orthopsychiatric Association), in a nuclear family with two parents, two children, and two sets of grandparents, there are 28 possible pairs and 247 potential groupings between and among people. Looking at a stepfamily with two adults (who are each parents of two children), their parents, their ex-spouses (the biological parents of the children brought into the stepfamily), and their parents, there are 136 possible pairs and 136,954 groupings of people. Yet, in spite of the potential, children are often more isolated in stepfamilies.

The scenario just described does not include any of the parents' brothers or sisters who may also be called upon. Sometimes it's just a matter of letting them know their presence is valued and giving them a chance to become well acquainted with the children. Betty, a Toronto stepmother, found it took just a little initiative on her part to help establish a pattern. Her husband Lorne's brother and sister-in-law in Kingston extended warm welcomes but did not think to make the first move in inviting the two children, Anne, 8, and Jason, 6, to come for an overnight visit. So Betty and Lorne began visiting Kingston several times a year, staying at a motel while the children stayed with their aunt and uncle and cousins. From this early experience has grown a bond among all the children, and a special sense of belonging for Anne and Jason in their aunt and uncle's home. Once she had made the initial move, Betty was able to withdraw a little. Now that the children are teenagers, they believe this strong bond with their relatives always existed. The aunt and uncle say they wish they had thought even earlier about their role in the children's lives.

Understanding that each family member retains loyalties to others outside the stepfamily home, and appreciating the variety in each other's background are the first steps to establishing new relationships within that new circle. Far from detracting from the strength and vitality of the stepfamily, the more caring contacts the children have, the richer and more satisfying life within the stepfamily can become.

Although it is not common for a child who stays with his grandparents at the time of divorce to remain with them when a parent remarries, in some cases, with a lot of love and good will, it works beautifully. Jan is 14 now, and has lived with her grandmother in Regina since she was one year old. Her young parents divorced at that time, and her mother moved to Montreal. Although Jan lives with her father's mother, she still keeps in touch with her mother through letters. Recently, Jan's father remarried. Jan participated fully in the family celebration, and welcomed the woman who is now her stepmother. However, she will continue to live with her grandmother while making frequent visits to her father and his new home, thus continuing an established living pattern that is very positive for her.

In the end, it comes down to specific people and situations. What would you do if you were a part of these families?

1. Seven-year-old Anne lives with her father and her stepmother. The stepmother is a manager in a large company and finds it very difficult to leave work at short notice. When Anne comes down with the flu, and neither the father nor stepmother can leave their jobs, what should they do? Should the stepmother contact the little girl's aunt or her natural mother who is working part-time and has more flexible working hours?

2. When Tom remarried, he stubbornly insisted that his first wife's family should give up their interest in his children who were eight, 10 and 12. To reinforce this idea, he even made the children send back birthday cards and Christmas gifts. What could a concerned relative of the children's natural mother do to re-establish the bond with the children? Could the new stepmother be an ally in getting the children in touch with their aunts and cousins?

3. When Janet married John, she expected to have the opportunity to spend some time with him alone. Both their sets of children from previous marriages live with them. However, Janet's former husband always has his children for a month every summer. Now John's former wife has remarried, and she and her husband have a cottage a few hours' drive from the stepfamily's home. But they have never invited her children even for a weekend, so when Janet's children are away, John's are still always at home. Janet would like a bit more privacy and she wants the children to visit more with their natural mother. It does not look like anyone else is going to make a move. Should Janet contact the natural mother and suggest that she invite her children over to the cottage?

Recommendations

	Don't	Do
General	Don't isolate the children from potentially supportive adults.	Allow children the flexibility to move back and forth between families.

	Don't	**Do**
Custodial parent (father)	Don't feel you must protect your child from all experiences outside your own boundaries. Overprotection allows the child to have unrealistic expectations.	Allow and facilitate continued relationships.
	Don't keep the children away from their extended family as a way of getting back at your spouse.	Do separate your own unresolved feelings from the children's need.
Stepparent (mother)	Don't expect instant love from your family for the children or vice versa.	Establish new roles very slowly.
Natural mother	Don't put your children into a loyalty bind.	Help your own family continue the relationship with the children.
Children	Don't reject supportive adults out of loyalty to one parent.	Recognize that different people can care for you in different ways, and that you can benefit from accepting all the help you can get.
New Couple	Don't set up loyalty conflicts for the children.	Encourage the continuity of family contacts and the involvement in your children's lives of those family members who are willing and able to make a positive contribution.

Chapter Five

Discipline

"It's a lot like trying to run a ship", says Noreen, a Vancouver high school teacher who loves to get out on the water on summer weekends. "If you think you can live in a stepfamily with no rules or responsibilities, you're crazy, and you'll never get anywhere. But everybody has to understand what the rules are and what the words mean. That's the only way to get some smooth sailing out of all that hard work."

Noreen should know. For five years now, she and her husband Sam have been working out rules and schedules for a household that includes her two teenage sons from a previous marriage, and his son and daughter, aged 10 and 12, from his first marriage.

Discipline involves setting reasonable limits on behavior. It is not a tool stepmothers can use to vent their frustration at their partner's children. Most of all, it is surely not an incidental matter that both partners can safely leave until the children have adjusted to a new household. Establishing rules and a routine are part of the adjustment process as well as disciplinary factor.

Maintaining discipline is an adult responsibility aimed at preparing children to face the world equipped to manage their lives. It works best in any household when there is consistency and cooperation between the adults concerning their approach to the inevitable testing of authority.

Many books have been written dealing with the practical aspects of discipline. The best books link the discipline with child development. They recognize that a child's understanding and ability to follow rules and to function independently increases as he or she grows. Our purpose here is to focus on the particular problems experienced in stepfamilies. Of course, guidelines for behavior in any family must contain allowances for ages and stages of development. In a stepfamily, they must also make allowances for the effects of unsettling changes in a child's life and living arrangements. Many of these were outlined in the chapter on taking care.

Rules and expectations in a new household must be clearly defined and understood by everyone. This is not as simple as it may sound. Setting guidelines, defining roles, and agreeing on limits can be particularly confusing today because there is no single yardstick by which to measure appropriate behavior. Parents who are themselves the product of a confusing society are finding that it is up to them to establish order in the new home. Whether they are prepared or not, they have to tackle this vital task. A framework of discipline protects the stepfamily from life's stresses and strains and helps to ensure its survival. Order and consistent expectations are also in a child's best interest, particularly for a child who has already experienced the turmoil of his parents' divorce.

Many factors affect the smooth functioning of a stepfamily, some of which can take years to iron out. But day-to-day life goes on, and patterns of acceptable behavior must be defined that allow the new family members to co-exist. Fortunately, the things that need immediate attention are often the least complicated. It takes time to build bonds of trust and affection, but such things as reasonable bedtimes and other routine matters can be settled relatively quickly.

There are four major factors that make the question of discipline more complex in stepfamilies.

The History

To begin, the history of the previous nuclear family and the changes that accompanied the breakdown of that marriage will have affected the child. Those experiences will have a direct bearing on the child's readiness to conform to the routines of a new family. At times, children of divorced parents have had to take on responsibilities beyond their years. Asking them to give up some of those responsibilities and, possibly, the privileges that go with them, such as late bedtimes, is not a simple matter.

Parents From the First Day

Second, the remarried couple are parents from day one. They do not enjoy the luxury of time together before children arrive on the scene. There they are, from the first day, along with some trepidation about the new adult in their lives. If there are two sets of children, the apprehensions are multiplied. At this point it is absolutely essential to talk things out. Having emerged from troubled relationships, remarried persons are anxious to avoid confrontations; but even at the risk of encountering some disagreements about discipline, it is very important to get everyone's feelings and expectations out in the open. A step-parent cannot be expected to play the role of a natural parent where discipline is concerned, but neither can he/she remain completely uninvolved. The couple must set limits and agree on expectations together, or the children will remain confused and constantly out-of-bounds.

A Place for Step-parent

Third, the new step-parent requires the natural parent's cooperation and support to be accepted as a full fledged family member with rights. When a new person moves into an already cohesive group, the group needs time to adjust to any new arrangement. In the interim, displeasure may be expressed in many different ways. One familiar form is to reject meals prepared by the new stepmother. The children must understand that step-parents have rights too, one of which is to be treated with respect. Since every family will have its own routine, depending on the ages and stages of the children involved, each couple has to consider methods of fostering normal development. Adolescents in particular respect adults who set limits and, without regard to legal custody arrangements, may choose to live with the parent they know will expect them to maintain a good academic standing. While it may feel "natural" for a stepmother to assume the task of taking care of the children, she has to remember that she cannot take on the role of disciplinarian without consultation. By talking about some of their values and assumptions instead of avoiding them, couples can explain to children their united approach to household rules.

The Non-Custodial Parent

The fourth factor that makes discipline a more complex matter in stepfamilies is the influence of the non-custodial parent on the children. Visiting arrangements that were in place before the remarriage can certainly continue, except in unusual circumstances, but one should keep in mind that visits will have an impact on a child's ability to adjust to the routines of a new home. One of the most positive things the non-custodial parent can do for the child is to encourage her or him to fully cooperate with the rules and tasks that are now part of his/her daily routine. Whether or not the child sees the other parent on a regular basis, the adults in the stepfamily cannot overlook this significant person in the child's life. There is no doubt that it can be difficult to maintain a calm, easy-going manner when a child returns from a visit with a natural parent who may be much more lenient, overly generous, or perhaps more emotionally distraught. But it's important that the visits continue. A child who has no opportunity to see his or her natural mother or father may express his sadness or sense of loss in the form of anger directed at the step-parent. Relatives of the absent parent can also help by keeping in touch with the children, assuring them of their support, and encouraging them to cooperate within the stepfamily.

All these factors have an influence on the ability of the remarried couple to help the children in the stepfamily realize their potential. It's a long, sometimes tiring, process, but it is so much easier when it's a shared task.

Starting Out

"It's tough to be the one who tells an eight-year-old to get her wet boots off the livingroom carpet when you don't feel you really know her well enough to be giving orders. It's even tougher when your husband and stepchildren give you the silent treatment for the rest of the day in response to your taking the initiative."

An Ottawa stepmother related these vivid recollections of being viewed as the wicked intruder, but her comments ring true to stepmothers everywhere. Anyone with children who remarries, or anyone who marries a person with children, is taking on a commitment to share the parenting. If this is not openly stated in so many words, perhaps it should be. Step-parents cannot substitute for the natural parent where discipline is concerned. Several reasons make it difficult for a stepmother to enforce limits on her husband's children. A child has little tolerance for orders or discipline from an adult with whom he or she has no intimate ties. Where there is a biological bond and a history of good times, then strict guidelines can be seen as evidence of care and concern. A step-parent, however, cannot fall back on the assurance that "we love each other regardless, and these bad feelings will pass." A stepmother has a fine line to tread. If she is too lenient, she can be viewed as trying to move in too closely and take the mother's place. If she is firm, she risks confirming the child's fear that she is bad. The dilemma can be compounded by the stepmother's own concern that she will be seen as a wicked stepmother. Some women avoid disciplining or reprimanding in an effort to be pleasant; they do not react, even in a most natural way, to obviously unacceptable behavior. But, if they do not speak up, eventually frustration takes over. They may begin to feel an all-encompassing anger toward a stepchild who is actually out of line in just one specific area. Speaking up about that one grievance may be all that is needed, as Ingrid, a Sudbury stepmother, discovered. Busy all day as a technician in a dentist's office, she realized she had to do something about her stepson's behavior.

"For the longest time, I hated to phone home because Tim always put on an abrupt, surly tone the moment he recognized my voice. Even if I wanted something started for the evening meal, or wanted to say I would be delayed, I'd avoid phoning and having to listen to him. Finally, I told him his tone was disturbing me very much. I didn't expect him to be friendly and chatty, but I did want him to be polite and less hostile, because it is important to know how to answer the phone in a pleasant way. It worked. Phoning home is no longer an ordeal, and recently I overheard him correct his sister when she answered him abruptly. I think he just hadn't been aware of how he was sounding. And it would have gone on and on unnecessarily."

When the new family starts living together, it is important to begin with first things first, rather than trying to tackle a dozen issues at once. However, it is also important that the step-parent not hold back or feel that she is unable to share the disciplining with the natural parent. Love and good intentions are not enough. The adults must discuss exactly who will do what in the joint household, and the new parent must clearly state her own needs and expectations about certain minimum standards of behavior.

As one 25-year-old stepmother put it, "You can't just wait for respect, because the longer you wait, the worse off you are. You can be understanding about why the children act the way they do, but you have to look out for yourself, and you have to tell them you aren't there to be insulted."

Children and teenagers need to be able to act their age in a protective, supportive milieu. They need to have an understanding of the ground rules, and know what they are allowed or expected to do. If the adults are not in agreement, or if the children are not allowed sufficient time to learn what the expectations are, problems can flare up without warning.

How to share

What are the options for sharing discipline? If both adults bring children to the new family, at first they may consider sharing everything equally, from finances to parenting. That rarely works, even in the most amicable of nuclear families. In a stepfamily, the member's past history makes it even more difficult. The close bond a natural parent has with a child makes it virtually impossible to share him or her totally with a new spouse. It is equally difficult to immediately feel at ease with children who share a family history with a new partner. Does sharing the parenting mean "I'll treat your children the same way I treat my children," or "I'll treat your children the way you treat mine"? Claiming equal treatment may not allow the flexibility that is absolutely necessary in a family of individuals with a variety of attitudes, experiences and needs.

Some couples hope to look after discipline in blended family by agreeing, "You look after your children and I'll look after mine." This may be unworkable if the intention is to become a family unit. There is a natural desire on the part of most family members to share basic values, hopes and plans. Moreover, the bulk of the physical care of young children and much of the guidance and direction of older children still tends to fall unevenly on the woman, whether or not she also works outside the home.

A third alternative is the one where the natural father sighs with relief and gratefully hands over all the responsibility for discipline to his new spouse. This will not work well, for reasons we have already noted. A step-parent cannot take over for a natural parent. Once a child has begun to trust the stepmother, she can help set appropriate guidelines for behavior, but once again, it must remain a shared task between the adults in the household.

Negotiating, sharing a portion of the disciplining authority, and keeping certain aspects separate for their own children are all necessary ingredients of a good plan. There is no magic formula that will work for every family, and there will be occasions when no agreement can be worked out between husband and wife concerning an appropriate disciplinary procedure. In the latter case, the step-parent may find that the most constructive step to take is to agree not to interfere. This does not mean agreeing to remain uninformed or to put up with unacceptable behavior.

Talk about discipline

Facing the fact that you and your spouse may have differences of opinion on appropriate house rules may be difficult, but not daring to set basic guidelines for everyone in the new household will be much more dangerous to your relationship. Without known boundaries for behavior, a child can constantly find himself in trouble and not know what he has done wrong. Making a child the scapegoat can divert attention for a time, but it will not solve the problem of two adults refusing to thrash out their differences on parenting.

An Ottawa stepmother in her mid-forties sought counselling when she realized that the anger she had been directing at her husband's children was actually caused by her disappointment in him for his lack of concern about his children. Three years earlier, her nine-year-old stepson had been referred for psychological help. He had difficulty keeping up with his class at school and at times was very aggressive. The stepmother was relieved when he went away to boarding school, but still she could not relax. She began to resent the stepdaughter with the same intensity, lying awake until the wee hours of the morning waiting for the 14-year-old to come home, while the father lost no sleep worrying. Disappointed by his refusal to discuss her concerns about the children's behavior, she sought professional assistance to work out the problem.

Another stepmother, only 27, was finally driven to leave her 40-year-old husband to force him to understand that his refusal to set any behavior standards for his two sons, aged 14 and 16, was damaging to everyone. Recognizing her inability to stand up to them without her husband's backing, the teenagers refused to obey her and delighted in tormenting her with practical jokes. After the boys purposely broke the music box figurine she had treasured since she was a child, she left, fearing her own safety would soon be at stake.

Where there are unresolved issues between a couple, it may appear easier and safer to focus anger on a child's "bad behavior" rather than on each other. Sooner or later, however, the couple must acknowledge their differences and find a mutually acceptable compromise for everyone's benefit.

Children want guidance

Setting limits is an adult responsibility. Children and teenagers need guidelines and boundaries, and they cannot establish them themselves. Drawing the line between adult privileges and responsibilities and those of children can be the most important first step. Some children who have gone through the stress of their parents' divorce and have taken on tasks beyond their years in a single-parent home have difficulty relinquishing their privileged role. For example, a teenage son has always taken charge of the family car when his father is out of town. Now, if a stepmother comes on the scene, does he still get to decide when the car will be available to others in the family, or does she? What about the teenage daughter who feels that the new stepmother is usurping her place in her father's kitchen? Can the stepmother count on her husband's help to make it clear that while the daughter's help is appreciated, the adults will now take final responsibility for assigning tasks? Very often children in a single-parent home have taken on additional chores and received unusual freedom because it suited the parent. But when such initiative goes far beyond the daily duties of clearing away dishes or folding clean laundry, children can quickly assume they are ready to handle situations or tasks for which thay are not prepared.

Nine-year-old Kathy was taking care of almost all her own clothes while she was living with her Dad, and she continued after he had remarried. No one took the responsibility of deciding what she needed, although the whole cast of natural mother, father, stepmother and grandmother would buy her clothing here and there, acting out a senseless tug-of-war over her wardrobe. Well aware that none of the adults were setting any limits, Kathy was able to manipulate the situation to her advantage. Soon she even took on the job of making the arrangements for visiting times with her mother since no one else was willing to take charge. With so little order in most aspects of her life, there is little wonder she could not be bothered to respond enthusiastically, let alone politely, to requests to finish up everything on her plate or to be in bed by nine o'clock.

While it is important to gear discipline to a child's age and stage of development, it is also necessary to keep in mind those changes children may have already had to cope with. Sometimes it is difficult for a step-parent to know whether children are acting up because they are angry or upset about the new situation or just because it's normal behavior for that stage of development. Behavioral difficulties can also stem from a prior situation where no limits were imposed. Now that there are, children will test those limits to see if the adults really mean business.

Other writers on disciplining children have claimed that what children really want to know is who is in charge and who loves them. Clear answers to these questions are reassuring to children of every age, although authority and love may have to be demonstrated differently to children of different ages.

Set priorities

No matter the age of the children when the stepfamily is formed, appropriate priorities must be established. Eating habits, for example, might be an area that parents feel must be tackled early on with pre-school children. However, in the case of teenagers seeking a calm environment and fairly strict rules about school attendance and study times, irritating table manners may have to be tolerated until the school situation is well under control. Trying to tackle everything at once will only create more tremendous tension and frustration.

During the first few weeks of adjustment to the new blended family, children can act in many different ways. Some appear unbelievably cooperative and well-behaved. Others, especially pre-teen boys, may show an increase in aggressiveness and be uncooperative. Parents will find it easier to cope if they quicky establish routines and expectations for everyday matters such as meals and homework. More difficult problems will be easier to manage or bring under control if the everyday parenting is going well. Serious aggression, depression, skipping school, stealing, or drinking under-age, need not be any more common in stepfamilies than they are in nuclear or one-parent households. However, the problem may be more difficult to deal with in view of the makeup of the stepfamily and the absence of a natural parent. If a stepfamily has laid a solid foundation of adult cooperation and consultation in matters of routine expectations and responsibilities for the children in their care, dealing with more serious behavioral difficulties will be easier.

At times, the reassurance of a secure environment can lead a child to regress or exhibit startlingly immature or obnoxious behavior. Among some children, this is a signal that they are dropping their defences and giving themselves a chance to catch up on some of the silly times they missed while busy coping with the stress of change. Adults are well advised to avoid overreacting to what may be a temporary phase. Although the behavior may be annoying for a time, the fact that a child feels free enough to try it is reason enough for cheering.

In brief

It takes time for a child to adjust to a new home, just as it does for adults. Keeping in touch with familiar people who care can make the adjustment easier for everyone. The non-custodial parent can have an important influence on children in the new household. One of the most helpful acts the absent parent can perform for the benefit of the child is to encourage him or her to respect the rules and guidelines of the new home and to be content and comfortable in doing so. Unfortunately, many children are denied regular contact with their non-custodial parent. Children who are deprived of the love, attention and support of their natural fathers and mothers suffer anxiety and distrust that can erupt in angry behavior and uncooperative attitudes. Also, non-custodial parents may prefer not to set any limits on their children's behavior for the short periods they visit, particularly if they do not visit often. At a young age, children may manage with more relaxed rules, but teenagers actually appreciate a home with reliable expectations and standards. Seventeen-year-old Steve, who usually lives with his father and stepmother, visits his mother every summer and always comes back with acne. He is well aware that eight weeks of soft drinks and sweets are the cause, and each year he complains less as he settles back into the healthy, routine diet of his father's home. Although he resisted strenuously when he was younger, he now knows that he needs some prodding to control his sweet tooth.

Adults in the stepfamily may choose to overlook the laxer discipline in an absent parent's home. Different bedtime and television viewing habits or extra treats are acceptable as long as children realize that they do not change the ground rules in the stepfamily. However, if the non-custodial parent plays a role that interferes with the child's adjustment to the new household, it is up to the custodial parent to raise the matter with the ex-spouse, both for the child's benefit and the stepfamily's. The non-custodial parent shares the responsibility for the growth and happiness of her child, even if she is no longer involved on a daily basis. When a natural mother can acknowledge and impress upon her children the stepmother's contribution to their lives, children will be more cooperative and content in both parents' households. The same idea applies when stepchildren living with their mother are visitors in their father's home.

The reward for setting limits and sticking to them throughout all the growing years includes those days that go particularly well for the whole family, and, in the end, participating in moulding a young adult who is ready to function to his or her full potential outside the family. The greater the number of people who get involved and feel some stake in this achievement, the easier and more successful life in a stepfamily will be.

Recommendations

Here are several things to keep in mind concerning one of the essential elements of family life—discipline

1. Custodial Parent (father)
Develop the habit of talking things over with your new partner. Allow her to share the parenting and accept that some rules and limits set while you were alone with your children may now need to be modified.

2. **Step-parent (stepmother)**
Looking after the children does not give you an automatic right to dispense discipline. Try to establish a routine and work together with your new partner in setting the ground rules and presenting them to the children.

3. **Non-custodial parent (mother)**
Recognize the need for new rules in a new household, and try not to undermine them by being indulgent or permissive on visits.

4. **All adults**
Ensure that all the rules are all clear to the children. Be consistent, be firm, and be fair.

Chapter Six

Special Events

"Well, no, I won't be sitting in the first row. That will be reserved for the bride's mother and her husband," Joan explained to the obviously puzzled minister. "I'm the stepmother," she added, as she realized no one had told him about the makeup of the family. "I'll sit in the second row and my husband will join me after he has given the bride away."

The church in which Tracey, her stepdaughter, was to be married was new to her, and the officiating clergyman had met the bride only a few weeks earlier. He was not introduced to her family until the wedding rehearsal. Explaining the seating arrangements for parents and step-parents was one more detail Joan had to take care of.

Since the stepmother is part of the household, she often has to carry out many of the preparatory tasks for special events such as a stepchild's wedding. The natural mother, however, has the right to expect V.I.P. treatment throughout the event. No matter how festive the celebration, a mother's exclusion casts a pall over the entire event. Similarly, a stepmother and her children have a right to recognition and an active role in the wedding party when a biological family gathers for a marriage. Honesty is paramount in any event in which the extended family, including step-parents, have a stake, and which requires pre-planning. It is important to be sensitive to *all* members who feel a tie to the family. Failure to recognize the complexity of a stepfamily can cause unintentional pain.

Consider a recent situation where a 50-year-old businessman died in a tragic airplane accident. At the funeral, held in a small town north of Toronto, the minister was aware of the presence of the suddenly widowed second wife and her own teenage children. He did not know, however, that the businessman's adult son and daughter from his first marriage were also at the service to mourn their father, with whom they had lived until their late teens. A close friend of the family, a stepmother herself, noticed they had not been acknowledged by the minister and found an opportunity to inform him following the burial service. It was too late to relieve the young people's grief that day, but in the future that clergyman *may* have been more sensitive to the fact that families are often more complex than they appear.

Weddings and funerals are but two special events that can pose particular problems for stepfamilies. Most persons are still oblivious to the possible strains such public occasions can generate. Few people are aware of the range of emotions that those involved are trying to control.

Special events in anyone's life constitute bonds that provide a sense of continuity. They are a link with the past or with tradition. Memorable occasions experienced by a blended family provide that family with memories it can look back on together and constitutes a part of the sharing that builds unity and emotional ties.

As in any other family, most such occasions in stepfamilies are private affairs that require less accommodation than those held in full public view. There are several ways, however, in which special events involving stepfamilies can be more complicated than in original, nuclear families.

First, more people are involved, including two sets of adult "parents." The absence of any one of these adults can be as conspicuous as his or her presence. On a child's special day, a parent can have a positive impact just by being there. If a parent does not attend because the situation is awkward or uncomfortable, a little girl's special moment, such as the day she moved up from Brownies to Girl Guides, will be marred by her feelings about the missing parent. Demands are high on everyone on such occasions. Adults have a special obligation to be as cooperative as humanly possible and to avoid diminishing the event by grandstanding or hashing out old grievances. Other members of a blended family may have varying degrees of interest or involvement in another's particular celebration, but their actions can also significantly influence the outcome.

Secondly, special events can revive or amplify feelings of loss for the former family and its traditions, as well as some of the frustrations and anxieties that are a part of the process of adjusting to a new stepfamily. Special occasions can evoke a sudden desire to share the happiness of the moment with a person who is no longer a part of one's life. For example, it is not unusual for a parent to wish that his or her ex-spouse could share his or her excitement when something special occurs in their child's life and the step-parent cannot summon up much enthusiasm. Children too will miss their other parent or specific places and people connected with their earlier life. They can even feel that celebrating happily in a new situation is being disloyal to the past. However, children can be helped to realize that sharing memories of good times with the new members of the family is much healthier for everyone than trying to suppress good feelings along with the feelings of loss. On the other hand, sometimes children will repeatedly recall happy times in great detail in order to remind the new step-parent that he or she was not part of the picture then.

Thirdly, although a special event involving a stepfamily can appear similar to that occurring in any family, underlying feelings and relationships can be explosive. There is often an assumption that if it's special, it should be a happy occasion. But someone must take the responsibility to try to make it so, and even the most careful planning does not guarantee success. There will still be times when a step-parent will think, "I wish this were really my kid," or when a stepchild will wish he or she did not have to worry about four parents. Wanting to change the situation will not help either of them, nor is anger the best way for a stepmother to overcome feeling insignificant at a family event. Longing for the original nuclear family prevents a child from making the most of his or her special day. All should keep in mind that a child deserves a day of happy memories, and do their best not to stir up loyalty conflicts.

If a special event does turn out to be a difficult experience, discussing it later may help, as can sharing the experience with close friends outside the family who have gone through similar situations. Since there are still very few guidelines for stepfamilies, the tendency is to automatically revert to familiar ways of doing things. Blended families need time to develop their own special moments.

In this chapter we examine special events that represent turning points in life: milestones, annual holidays and unexpected crises. They can all be memorable, and they can also all become very complicated.

Rites of Passage

There are very few special events that occur *because* of the stepfamily itself, but the remarriage of the two adults is one of them. Although it is the adults who make the actual decision, the children are usually included in the planning and ceremony.

There are a variety of ways in which couples may seek to make the event significant for all involved. They are not always "traditional" approaches; the aim is to make everyone feel from the beginning they have a stake in the new situation.

A wedding is a positive expression of faith in the future. It represents the hope that the new family will have good times and a determination to work toward that goal. Involving the children in that commitment by making them an integral part of the occasion lets them in on some of that hope and optimism.

Joan and Tom, the Calgary couple who recently oversaw the arrangements for his daughter's wedding, had taken their own marriage ceremony very seriously five years earlier. To symbolize the uniting of their two families, their six teenagers (four of his and two of hers) participated in the planning. The girls were bridesmaids while the boys served as ushers. It was an important, joyous day for all of them. The young people's wedding gift to their live-in parents was a studio portrait of their six smiling faces. It is still displayed prominently in Joan and Tom's home as a happy reminder of a cooperative venture.

For Paula, a Toronto magazine editor marrying James, an insurance executive, after a four-year courtship, it was a day of jockeying for position with James' seven-year-old daughter, Linda. Linda's smocked pink dress was made before those of her two older sisters, or even the bride's. In most of the photographs of the reception, the little girl appears between her father and new stepmother in what might be seen as a move to keep them apart. Paula knew all the children well. A few years earlier, they had actually invited her to be their new mother. But amid all the excitement of the wedding day came the realization that there is a big difference between

a stepchild's feelings about a woman as an individual, and the child's feelings about the same woman in the particular role of her father's wife.

There are other milestones: times when family members gather to share in the pride of achievement or to celebrate a change in status. Graduations, bar mitzvahs and sports tournaments are among these potentially exciting and happy moments. These are the occasions when it is important for adults to focus on celebrating and not on items of unfinished business. They provide adults with an opportunity to help make a child's day, just by their presence, and no difficulties should be allowed to spoil the occasion.

Even with ample time to plan ahead and careful preparation, it may be difficult to foresee some of the emotions the event can trigger.

For stepmothers, who are often expected to assume more than their share of the work involved, recognition and emotional rewards are still rare commodities. This makes it especially important for them to recognize for themselves the role they have to play. They are in a unique position to affect the outcome of events by remaining somewhat in the background and serving as coordinator and overseer. Then they can take some satisfaction when things turn out well, and not be emotionally torn when the event lacks the impact they had hoped for. It also helps immeasurably to have a confidante outside the family to whom they can express their frustration, disappointment or even satisfaction during the planning stages as well as following the event.

A stepmother should also take care not to blend into a new family to the extent that she gives up the people and pastimes that were especially important to her before the marriage. There will be special events involving her own friends or relatives in which members of the stepfamily may wish to join. Often special ties are fostered among people who are not family but simply enjoy each other's company. When a stepmother held a birthday celebration in Toronto for her father's 75th birthday, her stepchildren were quite willing to lend a hand with the preparations because they and their stepmother got along well. However, one of their teenage cousins became the most enthusiastic organizer since he had spent many happy summer days on fishing outings with his older friend and felt he knew him best. The stepmother counted this friendship for her father as one of the bonuses of her marriage.

Stepmothers should take a careful look around at, for example, a graduation ceremony attended. They will find they are not alone in the stepfamily category. There will be other students who are rushing about to accommodate a mother, a stepmother, a father or a friend. They too are hoping that all are enjoying themselves and that nobody's feelings are hurt. There will be parents who feel awkward or that they do not belong. Some will be haunted by memories from the past, some good, some sad. Everyone will have his or her own response to the event, but if everyone understands that he or she has a role to play and is prepared for the feelings that will arise, each person will be better able to conduct his or herself appropriately. The natural father, for example, takes it for granted that his wife shares his pride and sense of achievement, and may think no comments are called for. But there are still no words in our emotional dictionary to describe the identity confusion of being a parent and a non-parent, a relative and a stranger, and feeling proud and superfluous all at the same time. Since social and institutional patterns of behavior continue to be based on a nuclear family model, children may still feel awkward having to request additional invitations for the extra parents, and those parents may feel redundant in such a setting.

Some people reach a point where they decide to stop wishing relationships were different or more than what they are, and instead attempt to make the most of the relationships they have. This is what happened to Joyce, a business woman in Peterborough, Ontario. She had a very difficult time getting along with her stepdaughter Donna, who was 15 when her father remarried. As a teenager, Donna never missed an opportunity to remind Joyce that she was the outsider. When she married and had a child of her own, Donna appeared a little less preoccupied with getting her mother and father back together again. However, it was with some apprehension that Joyce accompanied her husband Andrew to the new baby's baptism. At the reception following the service, Donna appeared to wish to purposely annoy her stepmother by calling her natural mother and father to join her husband and herself for a family portrait with two-week-old Danny. Standing on the sidelines as Andrew's former wife was reunited with him for the picture, Joyce realized scenes such as these had been re-enacted in different ways for years, with Andrew fence-sitting and unwilling to take a stand. Rather than going along as she had before, Joyce told both Andrew and Donna that she would not attend family gatherings in the future. She found that asserting herself in this manner led to the beginning of a much more cooperative friendship between Donna and herself, one based on mutual respect. There are now times when she comfortably fills in as a babysitter, quietly and unobstrusively getting to know her stepgrandson.

This anecdote brings us to an important point. By being aware of the sensitivities of the other people involved, and by moderating their own expectations, stepmothers can be more relaxed about any responsibilities they choose to take on. They do have a choice. They can become involved to the point where they are comfortable and accept to go no further.

Stepmothers should not feel responsible, much less guilty, for the failings of either of the natural parents toward their children. There is no need, for example, to shop for the father's birthday gift to his children. A reminder or two is certainly in order, but children are rarely fooled by a card that bears their father's name but was not chosen by him. It takes a little practice for stepmothers to learn to stand back a little yet expect appropriate appreciation and respect for their efforts. The observer role may feel a little uncomfortable at first, but can prove to be very constructive.

Some stepmothers keep diaries or private journals that testify to this sense of standing a little apart, observing and provding assistance in these rites of passage, but not quite being able to share in them in the same way as a natural parent would.

Sandra, a North Bay, Ontario, stepmother of two teenagers wrote one fall: "Mark is preparing to leave for university. There is a need to help him feel ready to go. But I also must help Gary (his father) who is going to miss him so much. There is a very close tie between them because Mark is the first person ever to have needed him so completely. There is a mixture of excitement and anxiety and we are spending a few days together exploring Waterloo where he will be in residence. There is a sense of family behind him."

A few weeks into the first college year, Mark's stepmother was able to write: "While he was in high school, Mark was preoccupied with working out his emotional entanglement with Meg (his natural mother who lives in the same town), and there was no room for others. Now when he comes home, I am part of that family he comes home to!"

Leaving home is one milestone that can develop into a crisis for some families. Moving out may be part of natural maturation, of having reached a certain age, but in a blended family it may also be to spend time with the other natural parent, or to minimize friction in the household. On the other hand, at times, stepchildren are in no rush to leave home, even after they have begun to earn their own living.

Denise, an Edmonton stepmother of four and mother of two raised the question in her journal: "What do you do when it is time for your stepchild to leave home? You don't want to kick him out, but for every child there is a time to leave. Somehow, the stability of his blended home is a new experience, and I know he may want to enjoy that stability for a bit longer but enough is enough! He is 25 and has a good job. It's time he got his own place. I've finally tried to set a limit, but I'm alone in my sense of urgency. Neither of his natural parents feels as I do and it leaves me with a greater sense of impotence than if I took the same stand with my own child. No wonder they say stepmothers are wicked. Even if you are trying to do a loving, constructive thing, it can be badly misconstrued."

Not all milestones have to be hurdles to overcome. Where there are no latent conflicts, the celebrations surrounding such events can include extended family members without apprehension. When seven-year-old Jocelyne observed her first communion at their parish church in Montreal, the family members present included not only her mother and father but also the adult children from his first marriage as well as his first wife. The couple had divorced amicably 10 years earlier; Jocelyne's mother, Anne, had taken care of her stepchildren until they left home, and they all felt close to the child of this second marriage.

Attending special events organized by other members of the extended family can also be instructive. The experience allows a parent or step-parent to give some thought to the way he or she plans for events in his or her own family. A party given by an aunt or uncle may provide an opportunity for children to have a good time along with their mother and stepfather, or their father and stepmother, but the extended family may not think of or know how to handle the invitations. It is important to show

a willingness to participate in family celebrations. As step-parents welcome opportunities to take their place as authentic family members, others will gradually adjust to this reality.

Annual celebrations

There are special times over the years children are growing up when natural parents and step-parents must work out a schedule of cooperative sharing of the children's time. Some of these may include all of a child's extended family members. Sometimes a child will have a separate celebration with each set of parents. Annual celebrations provide an opportunity for members of a blended family to learn from year to year and to make adjustments as the needs of family members change.

The non-custodial parent's emotional influence on the child reappears during each special event or crisis. Whether that parent is predictable or not, and has a sense of responsibility or not, he or she has a very real effect on the outcome of an event. While it may make sense for children to have a separate birthday party with each parent, frequently the non-custodial parent's plans are not known until the last minute. The children may be asked to stay longer, come another day, or they may not be invited at all.

Birthdays can necessitate frantic rushing around from one parent to the other, as well as a party with school friends fitted in as well as possible. For the child's sake, adults should set aside other grievances and cooperate in making the day as special as possible. It may even be necessary to schedule activities over two days instead of trying to pack too much excitement into one.

Within the new blended family, there may be rituals that are important to one parent and her children but that mean very little to the other parent and his children. A blended family does not start off with a blank slate. It is both impossible and unnecessary to try to make every celebration unique to the new family, with no traces of former lives or the values attached to them. Stepfamilies come complete with extra baggage. These remembrances, which include some warm and even hilarious moments as well as painful memories, need to be sorted through by each family member. If everyone keeps his or her memories locked away, he or she is denying him or herself and family the variety and the richness past experience can bring to both the routine and special moments of a new life. By sharing ideas, participating in the planning and remaining open to new ways of doing things, stepfamily members may find that their annual celebrations are quite different from those of other families they know but that different means unique, not worse. The important point is that the festivities suit that particular group of people. If painting polka dot Easter eggs or cutting huge grins in Jack O'Lanterns make spring or autumn enjoyable for a family, that is what counts.

Since stepfamily members have acquired established ways of doing things, there may need to be some compromises all around. If his children never had nickels and dimes in their homemade birthday cakes and hers always did, what happens the first time a birthday is celebrated in the new household? Talk about it! His children can decide what kind of cake they prefer, while her children continue with their customs.

Since Christmas arrives each year with unfailing regularity, there is every opportunity to smooth out some potential snags. Unfortunately for some, it is precisely what does not work out which seems to become a pattern year after year. Only a conscious, determined effort to avoid these pitfalls will arrest the monotony of repeated crises; at times it is not obvious without a careful examination of the past that identical problems present themselves each year in a variety of disguises. Non-custodial parents who agree to spend a certain portion of the Christmas season with their children can contribute tremendously to the joy of the season, but only if they follow through. It is upsetting for everyone if plans are ignored and schedules rearranged at the last moment. One Ottawa couple who finally realized that they had to count on one event to compensate for the uncertainty of Christmas Day began a tradition of a huge Boxing Day party for friends and colleagues. Now they manage to keep the Yuletide season in perspective, accepting Christmas Eve and Christmas Day as they come, prepared to adapt to the needs of the children. Interestingly, as the children get older and begin to plan their own activities, they are pressuring their mother to stick to a plan as well.

At times a few members of the family may place great emphasis on a special day, while to the others it means little. A special day may bring back happy memories, so we assume that it has to be memorable. It is not necessarily so to others, but adjusting to that truth takes time and an appreciation of other people's values. At the same time, a family member who feels out of sorts or uninterested does not have the right to sabotage the happy feelings of others. There will be times when a child or an adult simply will not join in a festivity along with other stepfamily members. It's difficult not to view such uncooperative behavior as an attack on one's own value system and way of doing things, but more often it reflects the desire to recapture a nostalgic past and the happy secure feelings it produced.

Extraordinary Events

Events or emergencies may happen without warning. They too leave good or bad memories. Fears and feelings of loss are aroused when a child becomes ill or when a parent suffers a serious accident.

Emergencies involving children are frightening for adults, but when they involve adults they are usually a mystery to children, especially teenagers. Betty's husband Tony was involved in a serious fall at a Vancouver construction site. He was rushed to a hospital where Betty waited until a doctor suggested she go home since Tony would be in the operating room for some time. By the time she got home, she was worried sick. Betty asked one of her teenage stepdaughters who was home to stay with her; but within 10 minutes Kim announced she was going out with her friends, oblivious to the fact that her stepmother was in a state of shock. An hour later she called to ask Betty if she had "recovered from her hysterics" yet. Pulling herself together Betty acknowledged that she was calmer. "Then if you're okay, I'll stay overnight at my friend's," Kim said, leaving Betty to wonder how Kim could fail to recognize that Betty needed someone to be with. Not all memorable events are happy ones, and in a crisis it is difficult to learn how to help others cope.

There are other unexpected crises that can have a greater impact in a blended family. When a child is ill, often the stepmother worries about the practical care while the natural father avoids reality. When 13-year-old Jamie was diagnosed as diabetic soon after his father remarried, his stepmother Laura had difficulty ensuring he maintain his prescribed diet. Paul, his father, preferred that no one talk about Jamie's condition. Maybe he felt that the breakup of his first marriage triggered Jamie's illness or perhaps he wanted to face it alone, but as long as he denied the need for some restrictions on Jamie's eating habits, a health problem was escalating to a crisis.

At times a major event in the life of the non-custodial parent can become a crisis for the stepfamily, such as when a sudden job transfer necessitates special travel plans to allow the children continued visits. Also, a parent's illness, accident or operation may require that the children visit more often, leading to a need for some adjustment to the daily schedule at home. Similarly, a new baby may bring unexpected changes, no matter how welcome the event.

However important special events or ceremonies may be—and they are important—in themselves they are only a partial reflection of how well a stepfamily is managing overall. They are like images under a magnifying glass, enlarging and distorting everyday reality, but they can demonstrate to a family that a cooperative venture is indeed possible. A new protocol needs to be developed for stepfamilies because there is still very limited social awareness of the possible hurt and pain that can be avoided by following a few kindly, common-sense guidelines, and by recognizing that everyone has a valid role to play.

Recommendations

Special events keep cropping up. Here are some ideas to help them go more smoothly.

1. Accept the reality of the stepfamily. Recognize that the position of each family member has validity.

2. Ensure that all the adults who share a concern for the children, as well as the children themselves, plan together for annual celebrations and special events; in this way, all family members will feel they are a part of the new way of doing things.

3. For stepmothers, have an outlet outside the family which can provide a buffer. It allows you to do what you know is in the child's best interest for

an event; frustrations and disappointments can be vented in a supportive atmosphere.

4. Recognize that it is normal and acceptable for certain special events to be more important to one part of the family than the other. If the non-custodial parent of a stepchild gives him or her an extravagant gift on a particular occasion, there is no need to compete with an equally expensive present. Expressions of congratulations and a gift in line with your own means will be fine.

5. As a step-parent, do not go to extra lengths to cover up for a natural parent who did not remember or who did not bother.

Chapter Seven

Stepmothering In Retrospect

From the vantage point of several years' experience, stepmothers often discover that the family has been evolving around them. Although the stepmother role appears overwhelming at first, and ambivalence and hostility are not uncommon, time brings adjustments and a new balance. A number of authorities tell us it can take from four to seven years for a remarried family to adjust to the new reality. However, the child-raising years fly by for any couple, and step-parenting years are usually even shorter, so a tremendous amount of growing and change for everyone is compressed into this relatively short period. The remarried couple may have some difficulty during this stage. They may not have separated parenting and partnership role since the children are a part of the marriage from the beginning.

As the years go by and the children require less daily care, the stepmother's relationship with them changes. Her sense of place, of belonging, becomes established, and the feelings of helplessness and anger associated with the early days or years may be diminished.

There comes a time to look back. Good parenting is not easy and step-parenting is no exception. Rewards do not come in the form of a spontaneous hug or an I-love-you from the children. High school principals who acknowledge the contribution of parents at graduation ceremonies do not yet mention step-parents. For stepmothers, rewards usually come as a sense of accomplishment at seeing young people better prepared to cope with life than would have otherwise been the case without the stepmother's contribution.

Contemporary society has produced an increasing variety of non-nuclear family forms. Households with adults caring for adopted or foster children with whom they have no biological ties are now more prevalent than ever. When the children's well-being is an important part of the adults' lives, children usually thrive. Some stepmothers, though, find it difficult to accept that they never had a closer bond with their stepchildren than had they been foster mothers.

"Now I can think of my stepchildren as I do of a foster child who stayed with me," recalls one stepmother. "He was never legally mine—only placed with me for a nurturing, secure environment during a period of unrest in his life. I always knew he had his own mother and that some day he would go home. My expectations were realistic in that case. It took me a longer time to understand my role with my stepchildren. The instant love that was expected didn't happen for them and it didn't happen for me. But that sense of responsibility on my part, and their need for special care were both present, and maybe it's because of that we've developed a tie that makes them still come home now that they're on their own."

Given time and patience, frequently, as young adults, stepchildren come to acknowledge the contribution a step-parent has made to their lives; and step-parents who did not have children of their own come to appreciate the opportunity they have had to participate closely in the life of a younger generation. Years later, it is also possible at times to recognize that creating a stable home life for the children also helped to strengthen the marriage. Sharing times of crisis and moments of pride with the children's parent provides memories for years to come.

Through the ups and downs, it is wise to remember that no family has clear sailing every single day. It is nice to feel a sense of pride as children become responsible adults, but the stepmother is unlikely to be able to claim the credit alone. It must be shared. By the same token, she should not feel responsible if the children do not realize all their potential. Remarriage cannot compensate for early damage, and if conflict between the natural parents continues for years, some of the stress will affect the child. It is also possible, unfortunately, that a stepchild and step-parent never grow to like each other. That does not invalidate the step-parent's rightful place as an adult in the family, however. The stepmother may find herself re-evaluating the past years, and the father as well may be wondering why his expectations did not all work out.

"The most difficult part was for my husband," says one stepmother whose stepchildren are now in their twenties. "He was the one who had the illusion of replacing the original family. He wanted a Mom for his kids. He didn't recognize they already had a Mom, no matter what, and that what he needed was a wife that his kids could get to know in that capacity." A father may have to come to terms with the fact that things did not turn out exactly as he had hoped. His new spouse may not have accomplished what he secretly dreamed—fixing up his kids to respond to his needs. When the time comes to measure results against original expectations, both adults have to recognize that the stepmother has made an important contribution to his children just by her presence, even if that contribution was not entirely what he had anticipated.

Not always happy ever after

As the statistics on marital breakdown testify, a high proportion of second marriages do not work out. The pressure to fulfill the traditional female role of mother and caretaker can be one serious stumbling block which eventually leads a stepmother to resent the time and effort she has invested in children who may grow up and leave home without ever having established a satisfying relationship with her. Second marriages, like any marriage, are not made in heaven, and sometimes a couple must come to the conclusion they were not meant for each other. The presence of stepchildren makes a second divorce more complex. As one woman puts it, "I was a stepmother, and even though their father and I divorced nine years ago, I still *am* a stepmother. The children come to my house at Christmas. Their visits to me are separate from their relationship with their father, but the years we lived together made us very close."

Stepmothers may find that, no matter what they do, the stepfamily situation will not improve. It may be that the father has not resolved his emotional attachment to his first wife, the children's mother, and this ambivalence creates tensions. It may be that the children have been so hurt and angered by their parents' separation and ongoing conflict that they will not cooperate in creating a stable environment. Their behavior may be intolerable, and if the natural parents will not set limits the stepmother will probably be incapable of doing so alone. By trying too hard, she can become a scapegoat.

On the other hand, a stepmother may find she is really *not* suited to assuming a parenting role. Being a stepmother requires sacrifices. Perhaps staying home night after night or often being alone with the children are just too much to endure in addition to the cost in time and money of raising children. Women who resent the presence of their partner's children should not blame the natural mother or father, nor take it out on the children. Recognizing their own limitations and leaving the family may be far better for everyone than paying the high price of hurting the children or themselves. A stepmother's honest appraisal of her ability to adjust to the pressures of living in a stepfamily will benefit everyone.

Sometimes a child decides to leave the stepfamily, not because of any problem or unhappiness, but simply because of ties to the natural mother and some sense of obligation. Although it may be natural for a stepmother to feel responsible, it may be a situation over which she has absolutely no influence. For example, one 16-year-old stepdaughter moved out to live with her mother in a small apartment because she thought she was needed. The mother was very lonely following her release from a long stay in hospital, and the daughter felt obliged to set her own needs aside to "get mom on her feet." Another teenager left her father's home when he and her stepmother had a child of their own, announcing, "I'm not going to be a live-in babysitter." Three years later, still living with her natural mother, she regularly has her young half-sister over for weekends and enjoys the opportunity to be involved with both families.

The step-parenting experience leads to a better understanding of the effects of divorce and remarriage on children. As this knowledge becomes more widespread, children's chances of coming into contact with adults who can help them adjust to situations they did not choose for themselves will increase.

The Family Home

As time passes, children who live with their father and stepmother begin to depend on this household as their home. It is where they keep their books, and other belongings, where their friends leave messages, where they expect their favorite meals, and where they can turn for advice and support when they want it.

Happy memories reinforce this sense of a home base and favor cohesiveness. One stepmother recalls a particularly happy time that actually took place away from the family home, but contributed greatly to fostering a feeling of togetherness.

"Holidays stand out as a time away from the tensions born of loyalty conflicts. Getting away from telephones helps to prevent intrusions into this planned time together. One of our best holidays involved sharing such a tiny cabin that the three children, their father and I had to actually climb over beds to get out the door. We enjoyed sitting on the middle beds, playing board games, drinking our bedtime hot chocolate. Since there were several other families at the camp, we met them in the dining hall and shared dishwashing duties. The night we had a bonfire, the boys were so proud that we'd remembered to bring our own marshmallows from home.

That was one of the most relaxed, happy times the five of us have spent together. It happened when the boys were in their early teens, and now, five years later, they still recall that holiday warmly."

On the other hand, there are limits to the feelings of togetherness possible in a family that includes a step-parent. For example, the family's church pew may feel uncomfortable. Dad may still appear at ease as he takes his accustomed place, but the children may squirm. They would be right to say theirs does not look like a regular family, but they do not usually mention it. They show it by searching around the congregation for a friend who is "saving them a seat". Their reluctance to sit with their father and stepmother is obvious; everyone is aware of the unease in the new grouping.

"At times like this, I feel like I have an infectious disease that makes others want to keep their distance, even though they have to come a little close for the sake of politeness," remembers one stepmother. "I feel like saying I don't care to be with them. I'll go on my own. But, for my husband's sake, I pretend everything is fine, even though I know the kids despise the idea of all five of us sitting as a neat group. They appreciate me in their own way, and they trust me and feel comfortable in this home, but in their hearts they don't think I belong publicly in their mother's place."

Sharing the children

As long as the children live with their father and stepmother, there is a chance the natural mother will intrude in that home. She does, of course, have a right to keep in touch with her children, but this right can be stretched to the point where it is disruptive. The sudden telephone call, change of plans, or apparent crisis can all have an affect on the stepfamily that cannot be predicted, ignored or controlled. While most natural mothers never abuse their right to contact their children, others make their presence felt often and inappropriately. Unpredictability is one of the most difficult aspects to cope with because by its very nature there is no opportunity to plan a calm, rational response. Being caught unaware again and again is unsettling.

With time roles can change. As children become more independent, it is increasingly they who decide how their time will be spent, and what kind of arrangements they will make directly with their natural mother. The custodial parent or step-parent is no longer responsible.

When a non-custodial mother does not share in the caregiving role, children often learn to look to the custodial parent and stepfamily for the support and guidance they need and want. They then develop a relationship with their mother that is akin to a special friendship. They may share similar interests and enjoy each other's company, but the children may not count on her to set rules or provide backup in a crisis. They look to home instead. If the non-custodial parent does not remarry, or more sadly, if a second marriage should fail, often the child becomes a caregiver to the parent. This reversal role approaches that of a "minispouse" and can, indeed, interfere with the child's ability to later form an adult partnership.

Some families manage to attain a happy balance or equilibrium which allows the natural mother to acknowledge the stepmother's contribution to her children's sound progress. Although it may appear difficult to imagine in the stepfamily's early days, over the years natural mothers can recognize that their children still put them first and yet are doing well in many ways because they have additional people who care for them. While many mothers may not be able to express appreciation to the stepmother for her contribution, those who have had the closest ongoing ties with their children will be the first to acknowledge the stepmother's contribution.

One stepmother, contrasting her weariness with what she viewed as the natural mother's comfortable, childfree existence, stated resignedly: "Once the children grew up and were able to manage their lives, their mother came back to more or less claim them. Sometimes I feel a little like Horton the faithful elephant created by Dr. Seuss. In that children's story, Horton agrees to tend the bird's egg very carefully, but once it starts to crack open, the mother turns up to tell him she wants it back. What happens is that an elephant-bird hatches out of the egg, to the satisfaction of all the young readers who agree with Seuss that 'it should be like that'. Well, I know that some of me has rubbed off on these stepchildren too. At this point, I'm an adult who counts in their lives but we're still not exactly close because they are also part of someone else."

This sense of distance—of a lack of spontaneous expressions of friendliness, let alone affection—between step-parent and stepchild continues to be a dilemma for some. There is apprehension and hesitation on both sides in emotional situations, whether happy or sad. Even welcome-home greetings after an absence pose problems. The sensitive stepmother, conscious of the young person's need to retain this emotional distance, waits for a clue before moving forward with a hug or a kiss, or even a helping hand with the suitcases.

Adjusting

Just as stepmothers have difficulty relating fully to their stepchildren, so do children find it hard to express in words what it means to them to have a home base kept intact by a caring step-parent. One young woman, away from home on Mother's Day, rejected all the commercial cards and sent her stepmother a telegram just to let her know she was thinking of her as a special person on that day. "I wasn't the most appreciative kid, but now that I'm on my own, I can really understand how much you have done for me, and I don't mind saying so," she said.

Stepmothers have a big adjustment to make but their families of origin have even further to go to make inroads in the stepchildren's lives. One stepmother's mother expressed it this way: "I wanted to have an active role in my daughter's new family. Resolving problems took a lot of time and patience, but I didn't want her solving my problems with the stepchildren for me. Maybe because I am a teacher, I believe adults should be models for children and not reject them because they are troubled, but try to help them find their place in the new family. Even though there was some anguish in the beginning, now that the children are young adults I must say they are extremely kind and well mannered."

This step-grandmother is wise enough to understand two vital points. One is that time is an extremely important factor in working out a new system of relationships. The other is to look at the adjustments stepfamilies require from the child's point of view. It can never be assumed that a child will be grateful for a step-parent. On the contrary, a child can feel quite ashamed of such an addition and may require time and maturity to think otherwise.

Another stepmother, whose three children joined her husband's two in a new family when they were all teenagers, is well aware of the term "blended family", though she would not use the term to describe their family. "Everyone seems to have benefited from our remarriage, but our families did not blend," she says after seven years. "I think we were able to provide more for all the kids with our joint effort. They had the stability of a family atmosphere with expectations and individual recognition. My original dreams of everyone really getting along as closely as brothers and sisters didn't come true, but maybe that was not realistic. We have still ended up with a bunch of nice kids. Our home was the launching pad for them to move into adulthood. It's a place for them to come back when they need to, and in fact they do come in times of stress or when they want to celebrate."

The marriage

"If I'd known at the beginning what I now know 15 years later, I would have stepped in much sooner and more often and given my wife the support she needed in dealing with my kids," says one father, grateful his wife had stayed through the years his children grew up. "We had lots of good times, but if I'd known the tough days were all part of the normal adjustment that was going on, I think I could have kept my good humour better and we could have all relaxed more."

One of the attractions these fathers have for stepmothers in the first place is their manner of caring for their children. With the children grown up, stepmothers find that it is time to learn to see fathers as men on their own. The beginning of the marriage was somewhat like coming into a movie in the middle. Now the couple discovers what life is like with just the two of them in the house.

The children too are content that their father is not lonely. As one stepmother reported, "on Father's Day this year, my stepdaughter was out of town, but she sent her dad a lovely card and wrote 'I know Jane will make sure you have a happy day'."

Summing Up

Pausing to assess the past after the children have grown up allows everyone to see that while stepfamilies encounter inherent difficulties, and some of these may remain, there are also real achievements and opportunities for further growth and change. Some of these opportunities present themselves when stepchildren marry and take on new responsibilities. "When Valerie had her baby and I became a step-grandmother, I was asked to give the reception after the christening ceremony. Something made me say no. It was just one extra thing at a particularly busy time and I was tired. So the young parents held it at their apartment instead. Valerie's natural mother helped with preparing and serving the food. I was a guest along with so many other family members, and I really liked my new role. I think it worked out very well and the young parents enjoyed their new role too. Everybody loves the new baby and he's becoming a bonding influence for the family. As for me, I've stepped back from my constantly competent role, and it seems that's a good thing for everyone."

Step-parents are continuously learning how to respond to daily aggravations and opportunities. Through trial and error, they begin to resist the impulse to give more than the children need or than they can reasonably afford in time and energy. This may be the one important lesson to be learned in looking back over those busiest years as stepmothers. The need to constantly feel competent leads many people to take family life too seriously. There's plenty to enjoy along the way!

Some things are particularly helpful in allowing stepmothers to make the most of the experience. Breaking through the sense of isolation and sharing one's difficulties and perplexing experiences are most important. The good humour and support of other stepmothers can keep life in a stepfamily in perspective. The encouragement and partnership of the children's father is also vital. Continuing education on the special needs of children of divorce and information on stages of child development can help prepare step-parents to deal with specific behavior issues. When both partners bring children to the marriage, appreciating the spouse's efforts with the wife's kids helps the stepmother to develop more tolerance and patience with his. Encouraging continued involvement with members of the extended family can also help stepmothers share the responsibility for the emotional needs of the children.

Above all, there is a continuing need to bring stepfamily issues into full public view. A more realistic appreciation of the challenges they face can help stepmothers, stepchildren and other family members develop comfortable and more meaningful relationships, to everyone's benefit.

EPILOGUE

There are joys and opportunities for learning within a stepfamily that can be among the most enriching and rewarding of adult experiences. In this book we have emphasized the ongoing contributions many persons can make to the family. In addition to the stepmother, they include the natural parents and the extended family and friends whose support is invaluable during the difficult process of divorce and adjustment to remarriage. Much pain can be avoided or diminished with a more realistic approach to life in a new family. Our aim has been to provide new insights into this reality, and we hope that these insights will make it possible for family members to adopt a more light-hearted approach to day-to-day living.

Knowing that each stepfamily's struggle is shared by thousands of others may provide such families with an increased awareness of their pioneering role in establishing the stepfamily as a healthy, legitimate, publicly-recognized family form. Such families also call into question the traditional view of women as all-knowing, all-inclusive caregivers, since a stepmother alone is not likely to resolve the difficulties in stepfamilies. Neither the natural father nor his children can be miraculously re-inserted into a traditional nuclear family form, no matter how much they might like to think so. Stepmothers cannot fill everyone's needs and still retain their own individuality. Although the father may pressure his new wife to be the perfect mother to his children, it is important for everyone's sake for her to resist such attempts.

Despite the difficulties involved, stepfamilies provide both adults and children with a family affiliation that allows them to develop as autonomous individuals, and the stepmother is often the key person in establishing this secure home base. To play this role, as we have seen, requires that first and foremost she consider herself as primarily her husband's marital partner, and secondly as a concerned adult in the children's lives, not as a replacement for their mother, no matter how great the children's emotional needs.

The change from a single-parent family to a stepfamily takes several years of adjustment for both adults and children. Understanding that life can never again be the same as in a nuclear family will assist rather than hinder this adjustment. The non-custodial parent will continue to have an important influence on the children, so the more cooperative the adults' relationship can be, the easier it will be for the children to adapt to life with a step-parent.

Most children are adversely affected by divorce, and continued hostility between the natural parents can result in continuing stress and pain for the children. The greater the number of persons who can contribute to providing them with a sense of belonging and self-worth, the better. Natural parents, extended family and any new adult coming into these children's lives can all help them in their quest for stability and identity. It's quite a challenge, but it can make a big difference, and it does not have to be grim.

Step-parenting is too big a challenge to take on without ample support. Finding others with whom to share the ups and downs, the frustrations and successes, helps to keep the family experience in perspective. It provides an opportunity to compare notes and check progress.

Stepmothers have their rights as well. With experience, they learn to anticipate the situations that can cause them emotional pain and can better prepare themselves to cope with the pangs of anger or sadness. Experience also teaches them that talking about the difficulties they face with other stepfamily members helps everyone involved to work them out.

We did not set out to write a textbook. Instead, our aim has been to bring the difficulties stepmothers face into full public view so the reasons they have historically been viewed as "wicked" can be appreciated for what they are. We extend an open invitation to all members of society to realistically assess and understand the reality of their situation and the contribution they make.

As more and more stepmothers look for opportunities to share some of their most difficult moments with others who understand, more support groups will spring up across the country. Those looking for one now can begin by checking the phone book for a Family Service Centre. Or they can start a group themselves, by asking friends and colleagues to join in. At first it may feel awkward or disloyal to disclose some of the tumultuous goings-on in your household, but the anger and sadness evoked by recounting such episodes evaporates as soon as another step-parent says, "I know exactly what you're talking about!"

Annotated Bibliography

Berman, Claire. *Making It As a Step-parent: New Roles/New Rules*. New York: Bantam Books, 1980.
A journalist, Berman is able to draw on interviews from hundreds of families to identify distinctive issues that confront the millions of families struggling with their new lifestyle.

Bowerman, C.E. and Irish, D.P. "Some Relationships of Stepchildren to their Parents," in *Journal of Marriage and Family Living*, May, 1962.
This is an analysis of questionnaire data collected from 2,145 teenage stepchildren. It concluded that "stepmothers have more difficult roles than do stepfathers" because children tend to reject father-stepmother families. While in the 19th century children usually acquired stepmothers through the death of their natural mother, late 20th century stepmothers are more often acquired through the divorce of the biological parents.

Bradley, B. *Where Do I Belong? A Kid's Guide to Stepfamilies*. Addison-Wesley Publishing, 1982.
For children, 10 to 14 years old, an easy-to-read, clear and helpful guide. Starting from the divorce, it focuses on the children's feelings at every stage and suggests different ways to deal with them. The step-parent's perspective, and difficulties in adjusting, are also described for the child. Several suggestions are made to ease tensions, share feelings, and communicate distress.

Engebretson, J.C. "Stepmothers as First-Time Parents: Their Needs and Problems" in *Pediatric Nursing*, November/December, 1982.
An excellent summary for nurses or other professionals to educate

first-time stepmothers "to be able to adjust to a new role in marriage with no cultural role models and with no period of pregnancy as a preparation."

Francke, L.B. *Growing up Divorced*. Linden Press, 1983.
Francke interviewed hundreds of children of divorce. She examined the children's experiences from infancy to teenage years. A most enlightening book for parents, step-parents and all adults who are concerned with helping children of divorce (in a professional capacity as well). One chapter, "Steplives, pitfalls and failed expectations," describes some of the painful difficulties encountered in stepfamilies as well as the causes for optimism. Case illustrations are well-chosen, and the particularly difficult position of the stepmother is underlined.

Gardner, Richard A. *The Boys and Girls Book About Stepfamilies*. Bantam Books, 1982.
This book has been written by a doctor primarily for children aged six to 12. It helps children understand their concerns with the remarried family and encourages positive adjustment by constructive actions. By understanding the children's perspective, parents and step-parents can better provide for their needs in the new family, to everyone's benefit.

Getzoff, A. and McClenahan, C. *Stepkids: A Survival Guide for Teenagers in Stepfamilies—and for Step-parents Doubtful of their own Survival*. New York: Walker and Company, 1984.
An optimistic, humorous, insightful book to help teenagers in stepfamilies with many situations—how to deal with parents, step-parents, stepsiblings, visiting, and more. Discussions of particularly painful situations as well as helpful suggestions and references to other books which may be of interest are also included. The authors are marriage, family and child therapists who are both mothers as well as stepmothers.

Morrison, K. and Thompson-Guppy, A. "Cinderella's Stepmother's Syndrome" in *Canadian Journal of Psychiatry*, November, 1985.
The role and stresses of the stepmother in our society are examined through the clinical study of 22 stepmothers. Their distress was found to be due to their situation, not to mental disorder.

Ricci, Isolina. *Mom's House, Dad's House: Making Shared Custody Work*. London: Collier MacMillan Publishers, 1980.
Dealing with the issues and ethics of divorce, the aim of this book is to

help parents reorganize their respective lives to accommodate the child's movement from one to the other. The "how to" approach provides easy reference lists and checklists. This is a child-focused book that will enhance the joys of parenting.

Roosevelt, R. and Lofas, J. *Living in Step.* McGraw-Hill, 1977.
An excellent book for the entire family, it includes case histories that illustrate the typical problems stepmothers experience in adjusting to the stepfamily situation. This book emphasizes the necessity of having a supportive and insightful husband. It also suggests with some humor that the stepmother should be viewed as a kind of "psychological and philosophical athlete."

Rosenbaum, J. and V. *Step-parenting - A Sympathetic Guide to Living with and Loving Other People's Children.* New York: E.P. Dutton, 1978.
A realistic introduction to an appreciation of step-parenthood —both for step-parents and for their partners with children. Some of the unworkable situations are pointed out to help couples at the dating stage to assess or reconsider their plan for commitment. Children's developmental needs at different ages are summarized and specific step-parenting problems and rewards are well-illustrated with stepfamily examples. Suggestions regarding guidelines for communicating are helpful.

Smith, William Carlson. *The Stepchild.* Chicago: The University of Chicago Press, 1953.
Enlightened for his time, Smith presents a comprehensive historical perspective on the role of the stepmother, which he claimed then was "usually more difficult than that of the stepfather." He attributed this to the fact that the man did not have to be with the children throughout the day. He found that the stepmother faced difficulties unknown to the "ordinary" mother. Even then he claimed that "overanxiety to be a good mother is often responsible for the seeming harshness and severity of the stepmother."

Stenson, Janet Sinberg. *Now I have a Step-parent and it's Kind of Confusing.* New York: Avon Books, 1979.
This is a delightful book that offers an explanation of remarriage to the very young child. Simply illustrated by Nancy Gray, it is a book to read together. It can be colored by the child to enhance his or her participation.

Visher, E. and J. *How to Win As a Stepfamily*. Dembner Books, 1982.
The authors, both mental health professionals, are pioneers in examining the structure and function of the remarried family. They are the founders of the Stepfamily Association of America. This is a highly practical, comprehensive book for step-parents. The outlook is optimistic and the authors' professional and personal experience with step-parenting makes their suggestions very valuable.

The Canadian Council
on Social Development

WHAT IS CCSD?

Founded in 1920, the Canadian Council on Social Development (CCSD) is a national non-governmental, non-profit organization. Through independent research, policy analysis, community consultation and information sharing, the CCSD provides a forum for citizen participation in the formulation of enlightened social policies.

The CCSD is the only national organization whose mandate and involvement embrace all aspects of social development and social policy. Since its beginning, the Council has been actively involved in the evaluation of existing programs, the identification of essential improvements, and the promotion of needed developments. It has been a positive, non-partisan advocate of social measures such as universal inoculation, pensions, unemployment assistance, workmen's compensation, medicare, legal aid, daycare, and social and cooperative housing. The Council played an active role in the development of the Canada Assistance Plan and the Child Tax Credit, and has been a promoter of the Guaranteed Annual Income concept.

The CCSD is not a "think tank". It is the only national social research, advocacy and policy organization with an open public membership. CCSD's analyses, opinions, research and information reflect not only highly professional technical work but also the active analysis and shared experience of its broadly representative membership.

The Council's diverse membership includes concerned individuals as well as representatives from business, labour, government, public and private service organizations, voluntary associations and institutions. An annual meeting of the membership reviews the year's program and financial activities. Council activities are directed by a voluntary 39-member Board of Governors. Board members are formally elected at the annual meeting for terms of one, two and three years.

The CCSD is a major publisher in the field of social development. Publications include: research reports and policy briefs; **Perception,** a bi-monthly, bilingual magazine of social comment and analysis; **Overview,** a quarterly newsletter reviewing current national developments.

The Canadian Council on Social Development

Membership Information

AS A MEMBER OF THE COUNCIL,

- you support work aimed at improving our social and economic environment;
- you participate in a network of other people sharing your social commitment;
- you are continuously informed of innovative ideas and major developments as they occur.

YOU ARE ENTITLED TO

- **Perception,** our bi-monthly magazine on social development;
- **Overview,** our newsletter linking the Canadian human services community;
- Preferential rates for participation in Council conferences and workshops;
- Information about new publications;
- The Council's annual report;
- Voting privileges at annual meetings.

AGENCY MEMBERS ALSO RECEIVE

- occasional free publications;
- two issues of **Perception** and **Overview**;
- other CCSD newsletters such as **Initiative** and **Crime Victims**;
- access to CCSD resources for consultation.

Membership Application

Name _____

Organization _____

Address _____

_____

Postal Code _____

Payment:

□ _____ $ Enclosed

□ Bill me

□ Visa _____ $

No _____

Expiry Date _____

Signature _____

Return to: CCSD Membership Services, 55 Parkdale, P.O. Box 3505, Stn. "C" Ottawa, Ontario K1Y 4G1

The CCSD is a non-profit organization registered under the Tax Act relating to charities, and tax receipts are issued for all donations and financial contributions.

Membership Fees

Individuals:

□ Participating	$40
□ Sustaining	$75

Organizations:

Annual budget

□ less than $100,000	$ 75
□ $100,001 to $300,000	$125
□ over $300,000	$200
□ Affiliate	$500

Libraries: $40

Municipalities:

□ per 1,000 population	$2.50